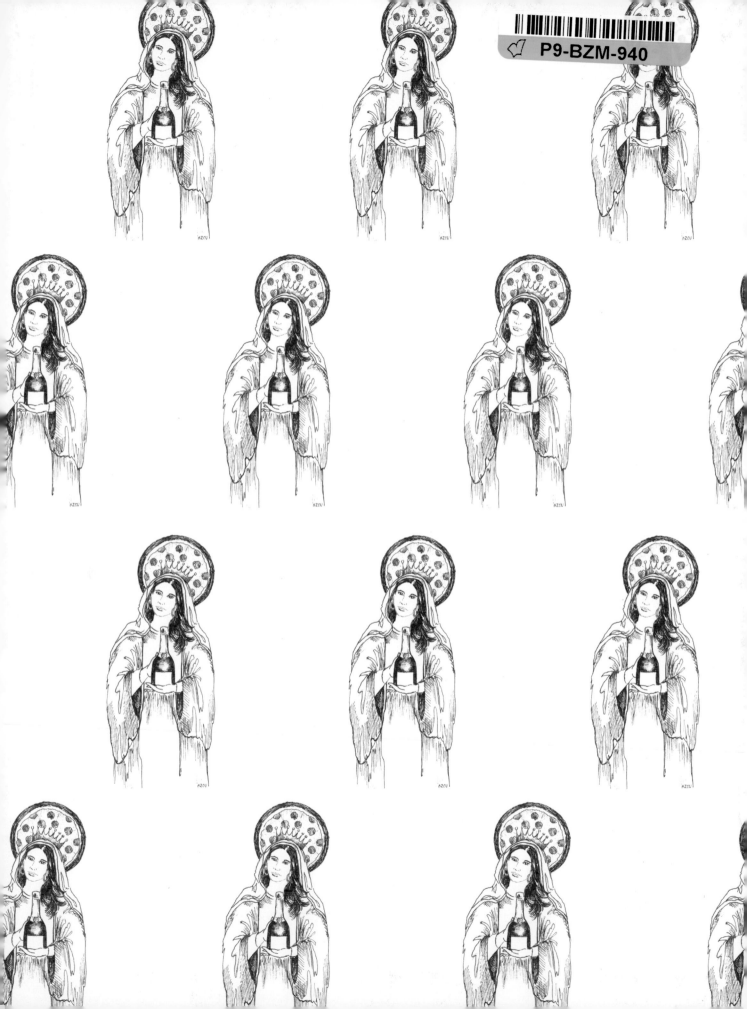

BETTER
WITH
BUBBLES

AN EFFERVESCENT

EDUCATION IN CHAMPAGNES

& SPARKLING WINES

ARIEL ARCE

UNIVERSE ◉

TO MY MOTHER, WHO
INTRODUCED ME TO
CHAMPAGNE ... WHEN I WAS
STILL IN THE WOMB.

BETTER WITH BUBBLES

AN EFFERVESCENT

EDUCATION IN CHAMPAGNES

& SPARKLING WINES

I BELIEVE A TRULY EPIC MO-
MENT—OR EPIC THOUGHT—
COMES FROM A DECISION TO BE
BOLD, DARING, TO TAKE A RISK.

—ME, I SAID IT.

TABLE OF CONTENTS

I CONSIDER MYSELF A VIGILANTE OF SPARKLING WINE, HERE TO SAVE THE DAY—TO REMOVE THE OLD YOU YOU THINK YOU KNOW

AND EMPOWER YOU IN YOUR FIGHT AGAINST MARKETING AND BAD WINE.

You must step outside your comfort zone and risk finding better bubbles! But as much as I am your Clark Kent, Lois, you need to stop falling off buildings and hoping for me to catch you. I am going to teach you how to have superpowers of a discerning palate so you can leap off those buildings and fly yourself!

CHAMPAGNE AND I HAVE SOMETHING IN COMMON...

This is how I feel
when I drink Champagne, about
three-fourths of the way through a great bottle. It makes music sound better, clothes feel sexier,
people look sexier, big ideas seem possible. It's a legal drug—
one that lets you get a little loose, fly high on effervescence, dance
a little too close, jump into pools naked. It's a mischievous potion that
can allow you to make some silly mistakes. And sometimes a mistake is not a
mistake at all, but rather a moment that will change the course of your life.
You may be asking yourself, "Mistakes... what's she talking about?" Let me
set the tone. Every bottle of Champagne comes from a singular mistake: the winemakers of Champagne, making still wine, had no intention of "tasting the stars," as Dom
Perignon once said.
In the mid-1600s, Champagne and Burgundy were at odds, vying to produce the best still
wines (without bubbles) in the world. But due to Champagne's colder northern climate, its
wines' fermentation would halt when temperatures dropped in the winter, stopping the conversion of sugar to alcohol. Once the spring came around, the wines would kick back into action,
igniting a release of carbon dioxide gas in the bottle. This produced bubbles—ruining the wine,
they believed—and the pressure caused the bottles to explode. (I picture corks flying everywhere
with Champenoise becoming the first non-pro dodgeball team.) They tried to fix the problem and
halt this process, until someone opened one of the few bottles remaining in the cellars, tasted it and
realized they had accidentally created masterpieces. I like to think of it as a positive screwup, and
now we have CHAMPAGNE!
**HERE IS MY MOTTO: Mistakes can be happy accidents, and happy accidents can change the
course of history, or just simply your life.**
My first happy accident was applying for a job in the business of booze. I was supposed to be
an actor. In fact, I was a professional actor from the time I was eight years old until I was eighteen. My mother was very proud of her triple-threat kid, and the first half of my life was spent
in auditions, dance classes, singing lessons, and competitive gymnastics. (Fun fact: I was
on *Law and Order: SVU* twice, as different characters.) I went to the "Fame" school for
high school (LaGuardia High School) and then the University of Michigan for a BTA in
Theater. Halfway through college, I decided to go behind the scenes in theater, film,
and television as well as take a stab at producing. I graduated in 2009, just when
the economy crashed, and I wasn't entirely sure what I wanted to do with my
life. I figured I would get a job bartending at night, and spend some time
reflecting on my future and deciding which industry I wanted to go
into. To my mother's disappointment, I never left the industry
I was in. That first job led to the last eleven years of my
career in the wine business. My mother used
to say I was making a big mistake—
was it?

I'm a believer in "fake it
till you make it." Just because you
haven't done something yet doesn't mean you
can't, but you also should be prepared to bust your butt
to prove to yourself you can! The reality is that you never really
make it: you just start learning, and you use everything you learn
to get better at whatever it is you're trying to do. I thought I was faking
it while writing this book until I realized I had over a decade of stories and
experiences in faking it that have led me to this moment. Because I had no formal
training in my industry, I made a lot of mistakes along the way, took some weird
turns, and made some "interesting" decisions, but, at the end of the day, these were all
learning tools for my toolbox of life. (Terrible metaphor, but you get the gist.) And Champagne was with me almost the whole way, my PIC (Partner in Crime) and my grounding
tool.

I love Champagne because it's alive. It has a story to tell. Champagne is the intersect of
Tradition (what you think you should do) and the Future (what you want to do). It is constantly
evaluating the past and using it to define its future. Champagne is rebellious and grounded, all in
one explosive package. It holds strong under pressure and lets loose as soon as it's opened. It's the
modern beverage for those of us out there trying to create something bigger than ourselves—and
trying to drink something that has existed before us and will exist after us.

The Champagnes I have fallen in love with (many of which are featured in this book) are made
by people who truly don't care about anything other than making killer sparkling wine. They have
all screwed up a ton along the way—bubbly with not enough balance, wines that never fermented,
dosing wines that didn't need it—but thank God for those mistakes. They are learning and growing,
and the ride has been beautiful to watch from the passenger side.

I have traveled the world to taste wine with bubbles, but no place have I spent more time in
than Champagne. My first trip was at twenty-two with my mother: two generations of Wild
Jewish Girls from NYC with no formal wine training driving terribly through the best sparkling
wine region in the world. What a mistake that was, because we got hooked on a place and
drink that would forever change us and our bank accounts. I am now thirty-two, and my
mother is no longer alive, yet I feel her energy and spirit in every glass I drink.

So here I am, a little more than a decade after I began, with thousands of
bottles tasted and ready to tell you all the tricks I've learned along the way (and
spare your taste buds from some truly terrible wine). I will also tell you all
the mistakes I have made so you can decide if you want to repeat them
for yourself. My favorite thing to tell people is, "Hey, if I can do it,
you can do it, too. Anything is possible."

WHAT IF ANYTHING IS POSSIBLE?

THINGS TO GET OUT OF THE WAY

Ever seen the Netflix show *Dark* or the movie *Memento*? This book is kinda gonna work like that. I'm not going to dumb things down for you, and I'll recap only enough so to not insult your intelligence.

Champagne is really hard to understand, because it's complicated. I am going to break it all down but it's gonna jump all over the place. Sometimes I will interject a thought, musings, my personal experiences, or technical information as well as references to sparkling wines from beyond Champagne. I don't want to bore you with too many terms up front, so I will explain and elaborate on these throughout my stories, because that's the way I learned—through just living it —and learned to love sparkling.

You shouldn't need to take notes, and there won't be a quiz. Your only homework will be to think about what you're tasting in the glass, decide if you like it, and see if it matches up with what I'm de-

scribing. And if you don't like what's in the glass, it doesn't mean you're wrong.

I hope this book will be a page-turner, and that you will walk away with as much information in my brain as I have to give. You can use this book however you like—there are no rules here—but I recommend starting here first and then visiting the world of sparkling wine. Champagne is the baseline for sparkling wine, and if you understand its basics (which are complicated), then everything else will seem like a breeze. I won't get too nerdy on you because I am not a nerd, but I am going to give you a snapshot of what's going on all over the world, and then you can decide how far down the rabbit hole you want to go.

Also, I love pizza . . . that's a tangent, but I think you should know that.

ONE GREAT GLASS

Before we start going down the rabbit hole, you'll need some things to enjoy Champagne fully. First: You need one great glass. (But I recommend getting more glasses because sharing bottles with friends makes wine taste better.)

What makes a glass great? The way it feels in your hand. Something light, not too heavy, and with a decent-size bowl to pour your wine into. Think of a small red wine glass—that would be dope.

Me personally, I love thin glass and a delicate stem. It just makes me feel fancy.

Side note: I am the person everyone likes to call "fancy." It used to bother me, but these days I've come to terms with it. I value nice things. I'll take quality over quantity any day, but I like to share, so most people benefit from my taste. I think a lot of things can make you feel fancy—even if you're currently wearing Chuck Taylors and cutoffs—and I think you can be casual and fancy at the same time. And having really light, delicate glass being the only thing separating you from a glass of Champagne is an attainable fancy thing and worth the investment.

When you taste Champagne, don't use a flute or a coupe. I don't have anything against these types of glasses, but they are not helpful when you are trying to pick up on such things as aromatics, flavor profiles, or textures. For best results, the glass should have a stem and be glass, so no plastic, friends, unless it's a red Solo cup, which comes in handy in a pinch if you're, say, on a fishing boat or in the middle of a field.

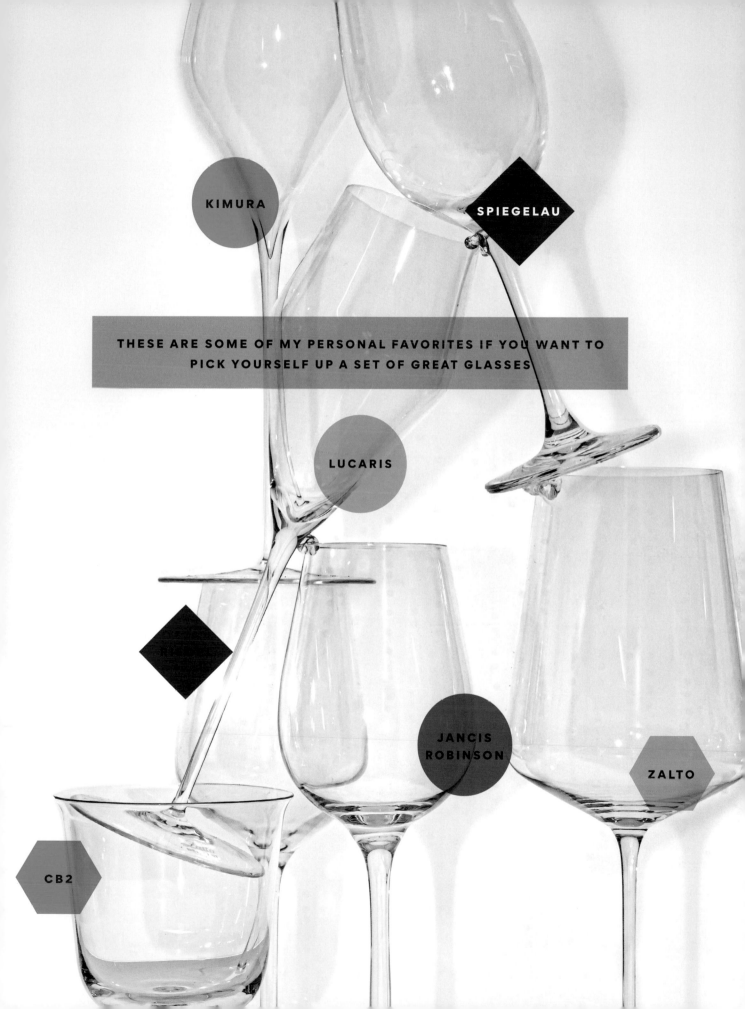

KIMURA

SPIEGELAU

THESE ARE SOME OF MY PERSONAL FAVORITES IF YOU WANT TO PICK YOURSELF UP A SET OF GREAT GLASSES

LUCARIS

JANCIS ROBINSON

ZALTO

CB2

At my spots, we take the same care with the music as we do with the wine—at Tokyo Record Bar, a DJ sommelier puts together playlist for every seating. Just as that great glass will make that great Champagne even more enjoyable, a great playlist that fits (and lifts) the mood will make those bottles pop all the more festively.

PAUL SIMON, "50 WAYS TO LEAVE YOUR LOVER"

THE ISLEY BROTHERS, "THIS OLD HEART OF MINE"

DEE DEE SHARP, "FEELS SO GOOD"

TORO Y MOI, "STILL SOUND"

PETE RODRIGUEZ, "I LIKE IT LIKE THAT"

LITTLE DRAGON, "RITUAL UNION"

JURASSIC 5, "CONCRETE SCHOOLYARD"

TOTO, "HOLD THE LINE"

MARTHA REEVES & THE VANDELLAS, "HEAT WAVE"

THE PSYCHEDELIC FURS, "LOVE MY WAY"

HALL & OATES, "PRIVATE EYES"

MUSICAL YOUTH, "PASS THE DUTCHIE"

JIMMY SMITH, "GOT MY MOJO WORKIN'"

THE BLACK KEYS, "LONEY BOY"

GRANDMASTER FLASH & THE FURIOUS FIVE, "SHE'S FRESH"

MYSTIKAL, "BOUNCIN' BACK"

MARIAH CAREY, "FANTASY"

TLC, "CREEP"

BLOOD ORANGE, "E.V.P."

TALKING HEADS, "THIS MUST BE THE PLACE"

STEVIE NICKS, "EDGE OF SEVENTEEN"

CARLA THOMAS, "B-A-B-Y"

NANCY SINATRA, "THESE BOOTS ARE MADE FOR WALKIN'"

LUPE FIASCO, "DAYDREAMIN'"

THE WILD MAGNOLIAS, "HANDA WANDA"

THE CARS, "MY BEST FRIEND'S GIRL"

FUGEES, "READY OR NOT"

1. Champagne is a wine. →

2. Not all wine is Champagne. →

3. Champagne is from the region of Champagne, France. →

4. Everything else is sparkling wine, even if it's from France. ↓

6. The three main grapes of Champagne are Pinot Noir, Chardonnay, and Pinot Meunier. ↓

5. This is not a bad thing. ←

WHAT IN THE WORLD IS CHAMPAGNE?

7. In Champagne, there are maisons who buy grapes from growers to make wine, and growers who grow grapes and make wine from their own vineyards. →

8. There are other scenarios as well. ↓

12. Champagne is worth the wait and worth the price.

11. Champagne takes a lot of time to make, and that's why it's more expensive. ←

10. (Don't worry— we will cover a lot of ground and things will be less confusing soon!) ←

9. There are some serious rules about Champagne, but there are no universal truths. ←

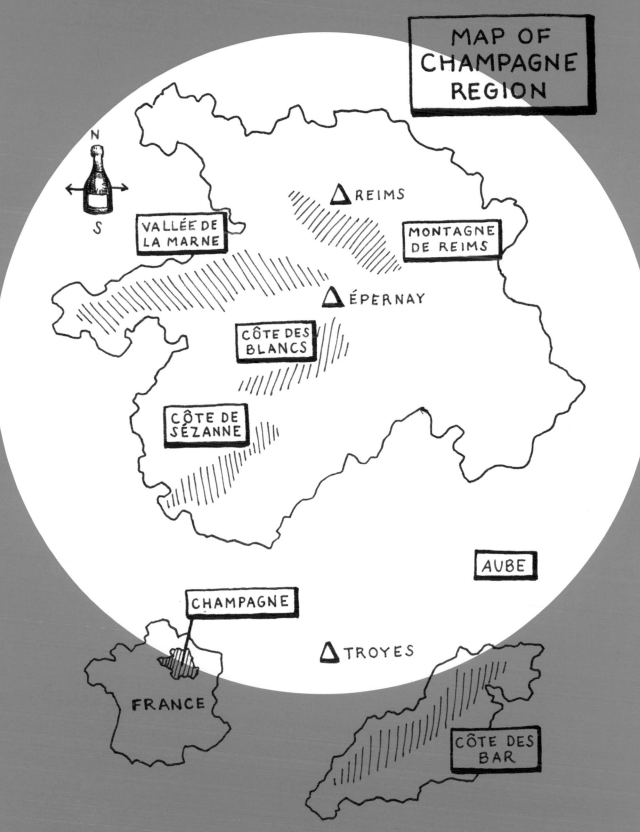

NO, CHAMPAGNE WON'T GIVE YOU A HEADACHE.

1. Yes, you can open a bottle of Champagne and not have to finish it.

2. Yes, stoppers really do work! (If you have the right one.)

3. Someone, somewhere, once said that you could stick a spoon in an open bottle of bubbly and it would save the effervescence. That shit is wrong.

4. Yes, you can drink Champagne at other times than New Year's Eve.

5. Yes, you can drink it with dinner tonight—shocker!

6. No, there isn't more sugar in a glass of Champagne than there is in a glass of wine.

7. Champagne is not made from Champagne grapes; it is, however, made from grapes grown in the region of Champagne.

WHERE CHAMPAGNE COMES FROM

The region of Champagne was once a large body of water, but then things like global warming, tectonic shifts, and 70 million years worth of pop cultural refrences happened—and now it sits firmly on top of a crustaceous formation otherwise known as CHALK. No joke, some parts of the vineyards could stock all the classrooms of NYC.

Chalk is what gives Champagne its flair. Fossils and remnants rich in calcite and lime over millions of years have developed into the foundation for Champagne's terroir. These minerals aid in the evolution of acidites in the grapes. Chalk has the ability to hold water for long periods of time, like a camel, storing moisture during long periods of minimal rain and hot summers.

Have you ever heard of the idea that for something to be unique and have nuance, it needs to struggle a bit? The vines in Champagne, especially in The Côte des Blancs in the south, have to dig deep through the chalk to reach rich nutritional soil. Their stuggle makes them work hard to mature and pull up the austere minerality which can aid in the development of balanced fruit.

It is the chalk's porous nature that keeps Champagne structured, acidic, fresh, and hydrated.

Within Champagne there are historically three main regions: The Montagne de Reims in the north, The Marne Valley in the middle, and the Côte des Blancs in the south. The Aube & Sézannais in the very south are the underdogs making a name for themselves! Each region is notorious for certain grapes and styles, but the beauty of Champagne is that every region has its own surprises.

In each region there are villages. Some are labeled with Crus—either Grand or Premier.

This system for labeling terroir was created in the 20th century after many years of uncertainty for wine growers who were selling their grapes to the large maisons. In order to maintain consistency, a percentage system for sale called "Échelle des Crus" or The Ladder of Growth allowed growers to receive fair prices for their grapes based on where they came from. In its origin there were 12 Grand Crus, and in 1985 five more villages were elevated to Grand Cru status, totaling 17.

Those are:
* Ambonnay, Montagne de Reims
* Avize, Côte des Blancs
* Aÿ, Vallée de la Marne
* Beaumont-sur-Vesle, Montagne de Reims
* Bouzy, Montagne de Reims
* Chouilly (Grand cru for Chardonnay), Côte des Blancs
* Cramant, Côte des Blancs
* Louvois, Montagne de Reims
* Mailly Champagne, Montagne de Reims
* Le Mesnil-sur-Oger-Côte des Blancs
* Oger, Côte des Blancs
* Oiry, Côte des Blancs
* Puisieux, Vallée de la Marne
* Sillery, Montagne de Reims
* Tours-sur-Marne (Grand Cru for Pinot Noir), Vallée de la Marne
* Verzenay, Montagne
* Verzy, Montagne

There are also 43 Premier Cru Villages.
There are no Premier or Grand Crus in The Aube or Sezanne.

In the modern era, this system is somewhat out of date, because now many growers produce their own wines from their own grapes, and just because someone has Grand Crus doesn't mean they make good wine and vise versa; some grapes from villages with no status can be beautful expresions of terroir or incredible winemaking.

MÉTHODE CHAMPENOISE

OKAY, WE ARE ABOUT TO GET TECHNICAL.
But not Too Technical.
(Skip to page 56 if you're reading for the drinking not the thinking.)

After a long growing season, grapes are picked at optimal acidity nine weeks after the first flowering happens around the vineyards in June, so September-ish. (Global warming might affect this timing.) The region of Champagne designates when each village is allowed to start and end harvesting. They have roughly two weeks in between. Some winemakers like to wait for more sugar to develop, leading to a riper grape, which can mean a richer and denser wine, while others might jump on the grapes a little earlier, when they are under-ripe, to create a more acidic style.

Grapes in Champagne are still picked by hand from the late end of the summer all the way to early October, depending on the season. This time is called the harvest, and it's BRUTAL. Thousands of pickers descend upon the region to help in the meticulous process of carefully picking grapes. As soon as the grapes are picked, they are rushed to pressing facilities to make the freshest, most nonoxidized juice possible.

Then, just as the grapes arrive at these facilities, they are immediately weighed, sorted, and pressed. I picture Kanye at a fitting. Like dayum, these grapes are divas.

Three successive pressings are permitted with each batch of grapes, but only the first two will be used by a quality winemaker. The third pressing, rarely used for a high-end producer, is generally sold off to big houses to use for blending.

Think about juicing an orange: You have your juice press set up and you cut your perfect Valencia in half. Then you push one half against the electric wheel. That first free-run juice is pretty clean, relatively no pulp. You pull the orange off the machine, but there is clearly more to be squeezed.

That first pressing, called the Cuvée, is what gets used for a winemaker's best wine. Out of the three presses, it has the best balance between sugar and acidity, a combination that creates the ideal freshness.

The second pressing is called the Taille. This can be used in blends and has a higher concentration of sugar and lower concentration of acid, which can make it less complex.

This is when you put the half of the orange back on the juicer. More juice comes out, but there might be more pulp and a small amount of pith. It's a bit denser due to the particles, and its freshness is slightly impacted by the additional elements.

Here's another rule. The CIVC (Le Comité Interprofessionnel du vin de Champagne, or the Comité Champagne) allows only a certain amount of juice per pressing: in a standard-size press, 20.5 hectoliters of juice for the first pressing (seriously, not a lot) and 25.5 hectoliters for the second (again, seriously, not a lot).

Going back to my orange metaphor, imagine how many oranges you have to squeeze just to make yourself a fresh cup of juice. Then pretend that those oranges are 1/20th the size, and, as grapes are more withholding. You try juicing raisins! It's a lot of grapes for not a ton of juice.

In the region of Champagne there are three dominant grapes, or the "Trinity," as we like to call them.

* Chardonnay
* Pinot Noir
* Pinot Meunier

That's correct, two out of the three grapes are red. Are you thinking, "But all the Champagne I drink is clear or golden"? Mind blown, right? More on this later.

Just about everyone has heard of Chardonnay and Pinot Noir. Pinot Meunier is a mutation of Pinot Noir and another cutie grape, Pinot Gris. Famously planted in cooler areas, able to withstand even stronger and harsher climates, Pinot Meunier grapes are often planted north facing. A large concentration of vines grow in the south in the Aube and along the Vallée de la Marne.

Pinot Meunier is starting to have its time in the sun, but for a long time experts deemed this grape as less age worthy than the other two Trinity grapes and worth less. It was seen as more of a workhorse grape for the region, but it's proving history wrong. These days, Meunier is causing a bit of a conspiracy theory—was it dubbed secondary for so long in order for big houses to purchase it at a lesser cost for so many years, filling their blends with Meunier and banking a higher profit?

I LOVE A CONSPIRACY THEORY!

There are four other varietals that can get into a blend but in total they make up less than 4 percent of Champagne's cultivation.
* Arbane
* Petit Meslier
* Pinot Blanc
* Pinot Gris

STYLES OF CHAMPAGNE

When talking about "styles" of Champagne, I am referring to wine made of either one particular grape or a mixture of grapes. This will get a little complicated, so hold tight.

Blended Wines

A blended Champagne is a mixture of two or more grapes, or what is called the ASSEMBLAGE. (So now if you want to know the makeup of the grapes, you can be fancy and say, "What's the assemblage?")

While the wines are golden in color, there might be one or more red grapes mixed with a white grape to create the assemblage of a blended Champagne.

FLAVOR PROFILES FOR BLENDED WINES
These are the flavors you'll generally experience when tasting blended wines, although different production methods will result in variations of these flavors.
* Strawberries and cream
* Ginger candy
* The smell of pottery or rustic woods
* Toast . . . and even burnt toast
* Yogurt with lemon curd
* Nut pie

WINES MADE WITH A SINGLE GRAPE

Generally speaking, Blanc de Blanc and Blanc de Noir—"white of white" and "white of black"—refer to wines made with one grape. But here is where it gets complicated: *technically* the terms mean that there can be Champagnes made from a blend of two or more grapes of the same color.

Guys, it's going to be okay. Once you crack a bottle of any of these styles, pour a glass, and taste, you will get it.

BLANC DE BLANC
"White of White"

This is 100 percent Chardonnay or 100 percent any white grape(s) from Champagne—but most of the time, it's safe to assume a Blanc de Blanc will be the Queen BAE Chardonnay.

Flavor Profiles for Chardonnay:
These are the flavors you'll generally experience when tasting Chardonnay, although different production methods will result in variations of these flavors.

* Granny Smith apples
* Stone fruits
* Apple pie
* Sugar cookies
* Creams

* Iced coffee
* Nuts
* Toasted bread
* Buttery brioche

Food Pairings:
* Seafood
* French fries
* Hot dogs
* Grilled cheese

BLANC DE NOIR
"White of Black"

100 percent Pinot Noir or Pinot Meunier, or a blend of these two red grapes. The Champagne pressing process ensures that the juice from red grapes gets separated from its skins as soon as possible to keep the skins from leaching any of their tannin or color.

Flavor Profiles for Pinot Noir

These are the flavors you'll generally experience when tasting Pinot Noir, although different production methods will result in variations of these flavors.

* Fuji apples
* Blackberries
* Blueberries
* Currants
* Cherries

* Chocolate-covered cherries
* Coco nibs
* Hazlenuts
* Cider

Food Pairings:
* Cheeseburgers
* Penne alla vodka
* Fish tacos

COMMUNICATING TASTE

Many people don't have a clue what they like, because they have never had to figure it out. Without realizing it, most of us drink based on marketing trends, gravitating towards the brands and buzzwords with big budgets behind them.

If I ask, "What tastes good to you?" and you say to me, "I don't know"... why don't you know? If I held up a red or purple jacket, could you not decide which one you prefer? (Being color-blind is a fair excuse.)

So let's take a moment to think about it...

You might find it incredibly difficult to connect the flavors you taste to a vocabulary, and that's okay. You might not have an amazingly discerning palate or know all the words to relay what is happening in your mouth, but that doesn't matter. You can learn. In the meantime, if you can't explain what you're tasting yet, feel free to talk in feelings or emotions or textures.

The rules here are THERE ARE NO RULES.

But, if we could start from the bottom, let's analyze our tastes.

WHAT WE TALK ABOUT WHEN WE TALK ABOUT FLAVORS

A lot of wine pros don't like to talk wine flavors because they think that if they tell a novice what they are supposed to be tasting, are they actually distorting the experience, and basically putting words in their mouth?

Well I say BS to that. I think when you're just getting started breaking down bubbly, you probably don't know the right words to use and definitely don't have a flavor vocabulary. Yet we all know what a green apple tastes like, or a piece of burnt toast. By tapping into familiar tastes, you can access a universal language for wine that can help you build your own vocabulary so you can ask for what you like.

You don't NEED to know that if you prefer a green apple to a red apple, you might like a wine with more acidity than sweetness. You don't NEED to know that Champagnes with a lot of toasty notes are often aged on yeast longer—therefore actually tasting somewhat like bread. You also don't NEED to know that sometimes earthy flavors like chalkboard chalk comes from the terroir that the grapes grow. All you need to know is which tastes do YOU prefer.

So here is a chart filled with the many notes I often detect in a glass of bubbly so you can see the true diversity of aromatics and flavors that exist in Champagne. As you look at this, ask yourself: Which do I prefer?

NOTE: We are not talking "dry" versus "sweet" here. That has to do more with dosage (page 41), or the maturation of the grapes during harvest. In Champagne, notes of strawberry can be dry while burnt toast can be sweet. So forget traditional associations between flavors and sweetness—a glass of Champagne can be incredibly layered, textured, and complex, and that's why we love it.

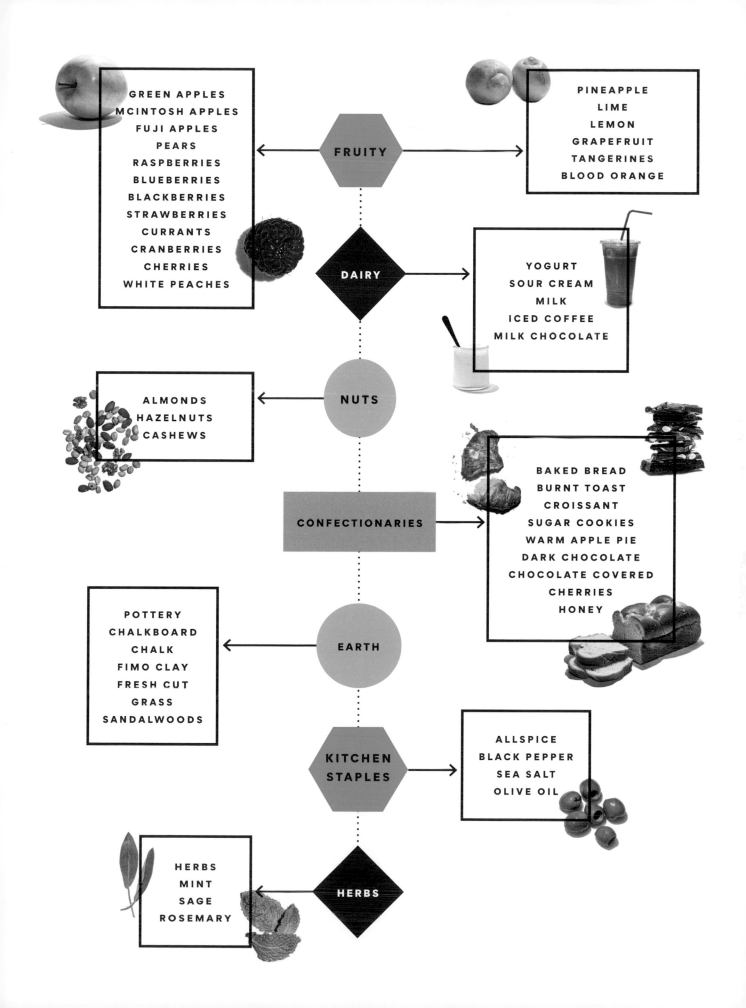

FRUITY

GREEN APPLES
MCINTOSH APPLES
FUJI APPLES
PEARS
RASPBERRIES
BLUEBERRIES
BLACKBERRIES
STRAWBERRIES
CURRANTS
CRANBERRIES
CHERRIES
WHITE PEACHES

PINEAPPLE
LIME
LEMON
GRAPEFRUIT
TANGERINES
BLOOD ORANGE

DAIRY

YOGURT
SOUR CREAM
MILK
ICED COFFEE
MILK CHOCOLATE

NUTS

ALMONDS
HAZELNUTS
CASHEWS

CONFECTIONARIES

BAKED BREAD
BURNT TOAST
CROISSANT
SUGAR COOKIES
WARM APPLE PIE
DARK CHOCOLATE
CHOCOLATE COVERED
CHERRIES
HONEY

EARTH

POTTERY
CHALKBOARD
CHALK
FIMO CLAY
FRESH CUT
GRASS
SANDALWOODS

KITCHEN STAPLES

ALLSPICE
BLACK PEPPER
SEA SALT
OLIVE OIL

HERBS

HERBS
MINT
SAGE
ROSEMARY

HOW CHAMPAGNE IS MADE

(see page 27)

FIRST FERMENTATION

After the pressing (see page 27) comes the *debourbage*, a process during which sediment or particles separate from the purest of the juice that was just pressed. As this happens, the juice chills and also *chillz*, which allows what is called the First Fermentation to initiate. This is when the sugar gets converted into alcohol with a little help from some yeasts.

This happens in all types of receptacles, from French oak barrels to concrete egg-shaped structures. However, to keep it simple, just picture the juice moving from the press to a stainless-steel tank that is kept at a cool temperature.

Yeast is important.

Think of yeast as a baker does: Some people spend their whole life trying to make the perfect loaf of bread. They go through tons of different strains of yeast to find what gives their loaf their signature style. We aren't going to get yeast technical here, but my point is this: whenever you are developing a technique to make something uniquely yours, you're doing what the best winemakers do. They think through every step of the process and try out different options until they find what works best for them. Some people will play around with indigenous yeasts, others with manufactured yeasts. Whichever one is used, yeast is an essential element to developing the characteristics of the wine.

At this point in the *debourbage,* you have a choice: to block malolactic fermentation or not. This is not an actual fermentation but a natural conversion of the harsh malic acid present in the wine to a softer lactic acid. Champagne grapes have a very high acidity, so some winemakers choose to let malolactic fermentation continue, giving their wine a softer texture, like cream or velvet. Others choose to stop malolactic fermentation before it starts.

At pressing every year, the CIVC (the Comité Champagne) mandates that every winemaker keep a minimum of 20 percent of the year's harvest juices or reserves, just in case. (You know, for the future, aka 401K.) Drought, rot in the vineyards, hailstorms, frost, extreme heat—Champagne producers have to protect themselves from disastrous loss every year and keep some wine for the future. (In millennial speak, that's a year of ramen and peanut butter sandwiches.) These reserves are comprised of what are called base wines. These bases, or vins clairs, just taste like very acidic white wines to even the most discerning palates.

At the start of creating their Champagne, a winemaker may choose to blend many different years' base wines, use one single base, use many different *vins clairs* from all over the region, or stay terroir specific. Depending on the different cuvées they produce, the wine can be a very complex blending process or a simple single *vin.*

SECOND FERMENTATION

BUBBLES, BABY!

After the first fermentation process and a blending period comes the secret weapon for the bubbles: SECOND FERMENTATION, AKA TWICE-BAKED POTATOES, AKA POMME FRITS, AKA THE DOUBLE-DOUBLE ANIMAL STYLE WITH CHEESE.

During the bottling process, or the *tirage*, a small amount of yeast (lees), sugar, and the *vin clair* are added into a Champagne bottle, sealed with a crown cap or cork, and then laid to rest for a minimum of fifteen months, or, if it's a vintage, three years. (Most winemakers choose to age their nonvintage—NV—or vintage wine longer.) This mixture is called the *liqueur de tirage*, and it's the concoction that's gonna get us where we want to go . . . bubble town.

PRO TIP: Some people really like the flavor profile of toasty or bready Champagnes. This can come from wines that have been aged for a long time on their lees—or EXTENDED LEES AGING.

Think about it: yeast is what we use as the base for bread. As the lees spend more time with the wine, it impacts the flavor profile and makes for more of a flavor of baked goods.

LET'S TAKE A BREAK FROM TECHNICALS AND TALK ABOUT WHAT NV AND V MEAN.

or Wines You Can Drink A LOT of
This means multiple years of harvest wines blended in one bottle. These wines make up the majority of the production of Champagne wines. They are the foundation of the region of Champagne and what most of us think of as Champagne.

Not every occasion calls for a super-sophisticated wine. Sometimes you want something that's a DRINKER not a THINKER. This category is massive and can feature everything from Easy Breezy Wines to Incredibly Complex and Dense Studies in Terroir.

Everyone needs to start their Champagne love affair in this category. It's where you can dive deeply into wines that are specifically curated for:

Single Varietals: One grape used to make up a wine. (Example: Chardonnay.)

Single Origins: Wines made from one Place. (Example: Le Mesnil using Chardonnay.)

Single Parcels: Wines made from one place within one place. (Example: Les Chetillons in Le Mesnil, which only grows Chardonnay.)

Philosophy: Organic practices, biodynamics, sustainable winemaking, and "natural winemaking," which we discuss in detail L8TR.

Rosé and Vessel Influence: Any of these styles made in different types of receptacles such as wood barrels, stainless-steel tanks, enamel tanks, concrete egg tank structures, and amphora clay pots.

VINTAGE *or The Rare Stuff, aka Unicorn wine, expensive bottles and special-occasion (or non-special-occasion) BUBBLES*
A lot of these kinds of wines need some passionate explanation because they are more than just grape juice and fizz. They can be very small production, but not always. A vintage Champagne takes a minimum of four years to get from vineyard to table and must be comprised of 100 percent juice from grapes from that year's harvest. The purpose of a vintage wine is to show the range of excellence and terroir of a single year's harvest. A *tête de cuvée* is a wine that a house or grower makes in what they consider to be an amazing year. Vintage wines have always been a winemaker's pride but plenty of wines have simply been covered up with marketing and packaging then slapped with a huge price tag. (The vintage wines that I provide a few pages from now put quality first.)

TINY ICE CUBE

After the yeast is collected in the neck of the bottle, the wine needs to be DISGORGED.

This used to be done by hand (skillfully, based on lots of experience) but now, almost all producers dip the neck of a bottle into a subzero ice bath to freeze the yeast. When the cap is finally removed from the bottle, a tiny yeast ice cube pops out. (There is a potential new diet trend in there somewhere . . . working on it.)

HOLD ON TO YOUR BUTTS, IT'S ABOUT TO GET TECHNICAL AGAIN!

A Riddle and Some Racking

Once a bottle is done with its nap/hibernation . . . It's time to get the yeast out.

A bottle starts on its side in a RACK aka RACKING. Imagine one of those A-frame chalkboards you see outside your local coffee shop, but with holes carved into the boards. This rack is filled with horizontally oriented bottles, each hanging by its neck.

In the olden days, the bottle would be rotated by hand clockwise a sixteenth of an inch every day until a full rotation was completed, with the bottle eventually resting vertically upside down.

This process can take up to two weeks until the bottle is upright and all the yeast has settled into the neck of the bottle. This process is called Riddling.

Now that we are in the twenty-first century, a lot of this process is mechanized in a large cage called a gyropalette, in which many bottles are automatically rotated all at once. This cuts a two-week-long Racking and Riddling process to just a few days.

There are winemakers, such as Marie Noelle Ledru and Maisons Pol Roger, who still do this by hand and their guys' forearms are BEAST.

DOSING—AND I'M TALKING MICRO

After the yeast is removed, a winemaker might decide to add a *dosage*. This is where a *liqueur de tirage* or an additional additive of sugar, grape must, sugar composite, or reserve wine is added to the second-fermented, bubbly wine.

Straight from the Bureau of Champagne so my facts are correct: *Dosage liqueur generally contains 500–750 grams of sugar per liter. The quantity added varies according to the style of Champagne.*

* **Non-Dosage, or Brut Nature:** 0–3 grams of sugar per liter
* **Extra Brut:** 0–6 grams of sugar per liter
* **Brut:** 6–12 grams of sugar per liter

Almost every Champagne we discuss in this book will fit into the above three categories. If you prefer something fruitier or even sweeter, look for wines labeled as:

* **Extra Dry:** 12–17 grams of sugar per liter
* **Sec:** 17–32 grams of sugar per liter
* **Demi-Sec:** 32–50 grams of sugar per liter
* **Doux:** above 50 grams of sugar per liter

A bottle of Champagne is 750 milliliters, or roughly 25 ounces. To put things in perspective, half of that, 375 milliliters, is roughly the same amount of liquid in a can of Coke (which happens to hold 10 teaspoons of sugar).

If 1 teaspoon = 4 grams, then a can of Coke holds 40 grams of sugar. So in a 750-milliliter can of Coke, you would be looking at 80 grams of sugar.

A Brut Champagne holds roughly 7 grams of sugar per liter. So the next time someone tells you Champagne has too much sugar, feel free to tell them it's equivalent to 1/11th of a Coke!

RECAP!

* Champagne made up of two or more grapes is called a BLEND
* Champagne styles made from one grape, 100 percent, are called BDB (*Blanc de Blanc*) or BDN (*Blanc de Noir*).
* A BLEND of a few harvests is called NONVINTAGE (NV).
* A wine made from only one year is called VINTAGE.
* NV takes fifteen months to age, while Vintage takes three years to age.
* The amount of sugar in a bottle is labeled as Brut Nature (0–3 grams), Extra Brut (0–6 grams), or Brut (6–12 grams).
* The three grapes of Champagne are Chardonnay, Pinot Noir, and Pinot Meunier.
* Racking and Riddling is the process of removing the lees (aka yeast) in a bottle.
* Dosage is the small addition of sugar to a bottle of bubbly.
* Chalk is the reason why Champagne's terroir is so special.
* Méthode champenoise is unique because it goes through two fermentation processes.

NOW LET'S STOP TO SMELL THE ROSES

(ROSÉ)

MORE DEBUNKING:
* Rosé is not just for summertime.
* Rosé is not just for girls.
* Rosé is really good with everything.
* Some Rosé even tastes like sparkling red wine.

Food Pairing
Think steak on the grill, arugula salad, chicken wings.

Rosé can be a blend of red and white grapes or it can be all red grapes or it can be all white grapes with some still red wine added into the mix.

Recently America has been on a Rosé kick—summer water all day, every day. Much of those Rosés are quaffing wine made fresh and young, but in Champagne, Rosé is most often the hardest and most time-consuming wine to make. But dayum, it's good.

MACERATION
The skins of the grapes spend
some time with the juice—aka
Maceration—during the
pressing process.

OEIL DE PERDRIX
French for "eye of the partridge." This
is a complicated process and few
winemakers use it as the wines can be
inconsistent. A little bit of color from the
skins is allowed to mix with the juice for
a short time to create a very pale, gloss-
ier / thinx /millennial pink pink. Not that
there is anything wrong with that . . .

ROSÉ SAIGNÉE
French for "blood." This is made in the style of red wine, where some juice is bled off and used to make effervescent wine. These Champagnes are structured and tannic and similar to drinking a sparkling red wine . . . a steak wine.

ADDING RED WINE
Still red wine made from the Pinot Noir or Meunier grapes from Champagne is added to white wine in order to create a blush before the second fermentation process.

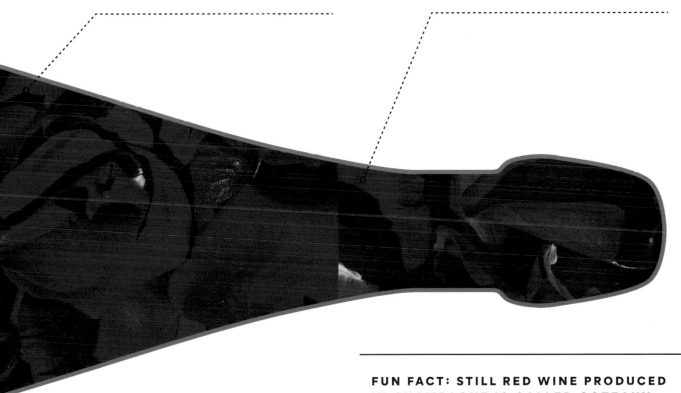

FUN FACT: STILL RED WINE PRODUCED IN CHAMPAGNE IS CALLED COTEAUX CHAMPENOIS. OMG WINE WITHOUT BUBBLES!!

It can be made Blanc or Rouge, plus a region in the super south of Champagne makes a still Rosé called Rosé des Riceys—Les Riceys being the town it's produced in. Coteaux Champenois needs more grapes to produce than sparkling wine does, and it's small production, so it's not often you see this wine. But there are some incredible producers of Coteaux Champenois out there, such as René Geoffroy, Gonet Medeville, Pierre Paillard, and others.

WHICH BRINGS US TO SOME BUZZWORDS: ORGANIC, SUSTAINABLE, BIODYNAMIC, AND NATURAL

HERE ARE THE BASICS!
ORGANIC is a regulated term, with farms and businesses needing to be certified that they are meeting organic standards, but note that many people follow organic practices without being certified. In the United States, if a wine is certified as organic, that means it has been made with organically grown grapes and does not include additives or sulfites. In Europe, organic wines must also be produced with organically grown grapes and not have additives, but the wines are allowed to contain sulfites.

When people hear the word "organic," it's often perceived as healthy, good for you, natural, hippie-dippy! But a Champagne that is organic can still be manipulated, preserved, and technically made and produced on a large scale. So rather than "hyper-niche," "organic" means a commitment to avoiding pesticides and other additives that are not approved by organic bylaws.

For a vineyard to be certified as "organic," a winemaker must rigorously follow organic practices for a minimum of four years. Many of the producers I highlight are not certified organic because the certification process is expensive, and they are small winemakers who don't feel compelled to get certified. But they all go above and beyond the basics of organic practice.

SUSTAINABLE
In SUSTAINABLE wines, winemakers have chosen to reduce their impact on the environment through means such as lowering their carbon footprint, limiting energy consumption and water usage, composting and recycling, and using animals instead of machinery. This may also affect how winemakers use supply chains.

BIODYNAMIC
A winemaker who makes BIODYNAMIC wine adheres to a philosophy in which everything is viewed as connected in one organism. Biodynamic agriculture can be guided by astrology, treatments, and farming practices that follow lunar cycles. The concept revolves around energy: the better the soil's energy, the stronger the vineyards will be.

Most people who practice biodynamic agriculture follow organic methods: they don't use herbicides and pesticides, they don't fine or filtrate with additives, and they add minimal to no sulfur or sulfites. They seek to cultivate a strong foundation of energy in the vineyards to create expressive wines with less impact on the environment. In a perfect world, the entire vineyard and winery ecosystem would be closed and self-sustaining, but it's especially complicated in Champagne, where vineyards are in proximity, so toxins from a neighboring vineyard can make their way into a biodynamic vineyard.

NATURAL
No Champagne is technically AU NATURAL, as the bylaws of Champagne effectively make the wines from the region "unnatural" (see page 124 for more on alternative methods for making sparkling). Yet there are plenty of winemakers in Champagne who are focused on organic production, biodynamic production, and natural approaches like spontaneous fermentation, avoiding the use of herbicides or pesticides, and not adding sulfur.

SULFUR
Let's move on from the "sulfites are the thing giving me headaches, not the alcohol" theory: All wines contain traces of sulfites, as it's a natural byproduct of fermentation. Sulfur is generally used to keep wine fresh and to fight off harmful bacteria. It's very clear when sulfur has gone wrong—wines will smell eggy or like an extinguished firecracker.

Sulfur in small amounts can be added to the grapes right after they are picked so they don't oxidize quickly. It can also be used to block malolactic fermentation and to preserve freshness in still wines. But in a region like Champagne, where many winemakers are converting to organic and biodynamic practices, sulfur is often used very sparingly.

There are no-sulfur wines, or "sans soufre" in French, and they can beat a wine of similar style. However, these wines are highly unstable and inconsistent, as they are easily damaged by production techniques, oxidation, and storage.

HEAD TO THE SOURCE

(HOW TO TRAVEL—AND TRAVEL WELL—IN CHAMPAGNE)

LOGISTICS Champagne is forty-five minutes northeast from Charles de Gaulle Airport. Book a redeye, pop two Tylenol PMs, and see you there at 9 am. (Traveling to Champagne by train is easy-peasy, but if you want to visit a lot of vineyards, I recommend renting a car.)

I can't stand to check luggage, so I pack light and smart and carry on—but I make sure to pack an extra fold-up bag in my suitcase. It's not unusual for someone to gift you a bottle of wine while you're visiting producers, and while sometimes those treats are better enjoyed in your hotel bed, it's totally legitimate to bring back wine in your suitcase. There are also some phenomenal wine stores and there are going to be wines you just can't find in the United States, so I always end up coming home with a bottle or two. There are fancy suitcases out there for wine, but I am a hot mess and never plan appropriately so I wrap my bottles in my clothes and hope for the best. Don't worry, they won't explode in your suitcase—though don't hold me to that.

DRESSING
FOR SUCCESS

If we ever get to meet in person, you will notice very quickly that I dress for comfort and the ability to lift twenty-pound boxes at a moment's notice. But I'll be damned if I won't look chic doing it.

This approach to dressing also goes for a visit to Champagne. It's important to present your best self—whether it's farmer chic or downtown hypebeast—but Champagne is still France. You'll want to bring a touch of class, but you don't need a three-piece suit to walk the vineyards of Champagne. I generally find myself in my NYC streetwear finest with an eye to the seasons: Champagne is cold in the winter and hot in the summer, and its oceanic influences allow consistent rainfall throughout the year, depending on the temperature.

And you can never go wrong with a brightly colored Hermès scarf.

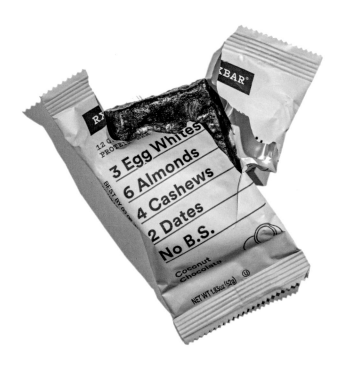

DOS:

* White sneakers (if it hasn't rained) especially in the Côte des Blancs, where the vineyards have a heavy concentration of chalk.

* Black sneakers (in case it has)

* A scarf, pashmina, or fold-up jacket: When visiting cellars, any of these will serve you well. Underground and sometimes many feet down, cellars are designed to hold a stable cool temperature, even if it's 90 degrees outside.

DON'TS

* Any form of high heels. (Though if you are visiting a fancy domain, you could wear a wedge or kitten heel or dress shoe to really indulge in the vibe.)

* A light-color pant: If you're gonna get down on your knees to examine a vine variety or check out the current varietal budding, you don't want to stand up and have dirt circles on your knees.

* Tight clothes: The people of sparkling wine communities tend to be very gracious. You might get very well fed, and you might get over poured. Either way, you want to be in for the long haul. Wear comfortable clothes that you can grow into over the course of the day.

SURVIVAL ITEMS FOR VINEYARDING

Pockets are key! I hate having a bag with me at any time, but a Bellstaff or Barbour jacket or a casual APC utility pant with pockets are good for holding:

* Pen
* Moleskine notebook
* Hair tie
* Scarf
* Credit card
* Advil packet (To plan for the inevitable Champagne hangover.
* Sunglasses (Ditto)
* Smartphone

WINE, DINE & RECLINE

As much as Champagne is all about the wine, there are also some amazing restaurants, bars, and hotels. I have been traveling to this region almost a decade, so while all of these places exist, some of them are newer to the scene. And if all goes according to plan, they will still exist twenty years from now. (In case you're reading this in the future.)

Remember how I told you I was a simple fancy girl? Well, I love an amazing hotel and Champagne has a few that I think are fantastico.

HOTELS

Hôtel Villa Eugene, Épernay
It's got a pool and French Victorian vibes.

L'assiette Champenoise, Reims
Three Michelin stars for the restaurant.

Hôtel Les Avisés, Avize
Owned by the Selosse family.

Domain Les Crayères, Reims
Old-world glamour meets five-star elegance.

Some winemakers even have B&Bs, like Doyard and Goutourbe.

PLUS YA GOTTA EAT AND DRINK.
North
* Le Coq Rouge
* Sacre Burger
* Racines
* Le Parc at Les Crayères
* Le Jardin
* L'assette Champenois
* Perching Bar. (Guys, it's a treehouse!)
* Le Wine Bar

South
* Sacre Bistro
* Kadev
* Les Avisés
* La Grillade Gourmande
* La Gare
* Royal Champagne

EPIC WINE STORE
* L'Épicerie Au Bon Manger
* 520 Wines, Epernay
* Les Caves du Forum, Reims

LET'S POP SOME BOTTLES

In my opinion, what I provide in the next few pages are some of the best Champagnes that exist, period. These winemakers are some of my favorite producers and friends. Together they run the gamut of flavors, productions, and techniques.

One of the many reasons why Champagne is so complicated is because every winemaker conforms to a different grape, style, mode of thought, farming practice, and traditions or new philosophy. I'm categorizing some together so they make more sense, while some are in categories all of their own. If you are like me and completely obsessed, I recommend trying at least one from each category at some point in your lifetime. If you're not gonna go big, just go home.

THE WINES

I pride myself on doing the hard work of tasting all the good, great, and not-so-great Champagne there is, so you can just drink the great stuff. Here is a selection of some of my all-time favorite wines, and also my favorite Cuvées from the producers I love.

It is rare to drink a Champagne for which the winemaker doesn't believe in something that strongly defines the wine, whether terroir, production techniques, aging in the cellar, or a vineyard-to-bottle philosophy. Generally speaking, a winemaker will have a lineup, or multiple Cuvées that they produce yearly or every vintage they deem exceptional. What I have been doing for more than a decade is tasting as many producers' wines as I can get my hands on, from the entire range that the producer makes, and then curating a selection of Champagnes that showcase the entire spectrum of the region.

Some of the Champagnes I have selected for these pages are wines that are no longer made, are hard to find, and are incredibly expensive. Others are entry-level non-vintages that are exceptional and everyday drinkers. Any one of these wines, I would sit on my roof and drink with you. Most of them I've drunk in cellars, in my bars, poolside, at the dinner table, on subways late at night, stranded at bus stations, in my bed, in my shower, with friends who had no clue what they were drinking and with friends who knew exactly what they were drinking. These wines make up my definition of Champagne, and they are the benchmarks I hold other Champagnes to.

GROWERS AND VIGNERONS

Many of the Champagnes I promote are made from producers who are farmers first—they spend the majority of their year in their vineyards. Some of these are growers and some are vignerons, or winemakers.

A grower refers to a winemaker who makes wines from only grapes that they grow. After the Second World War, many producers decided that they would take a crack at making their own wines rather than selling their grapes to a large maison. Not all of them were good winemakers, but they knew how to grow grapes, harvest them, dual-ferment them, and—tada!—make wine!

So while there are incredible producers of Champagne who consider themselves farmers first—focusing mainly on the quality of their grapes and the simple idea that great grapes can lead to great wine—a lot of the grower Champagnes we covet are made from vignerons, who have a very specific and technical mission for their final product.

A winemaker needs a north star, something that defines their style and drives them year after year to do the hard work it takes to produce Champagne.

The older generation of winemakers started with the question: How can I make better wine? A lot of them looked to their neighbors, like Burgundy, to understand how terroir and technique could enhance their Champagnes. While some people started the wave of studying oenology at university to learn about wine, a lot of how they learned was through sharing with one another.

Today's younger generation learned from these pioneers and many went to university as well. In addition, they have access to information in a different way via social sharing, their participation in established democratic clubs, and the magical internet. The region is even more open to sharing than before, and there is a flourishing trade in knowledge.

CLUBS

A fair amount of democratic clubs have formed in Champagne, where winemakers get together to talk philosophy, technique, innovation, marketing, and more. The most well known are The Tresors ("Special Club"), Artisans, Terres et Vines, Les Mains de Terroir, and Bulles Bio. Every April, there's a huge festival at which all the winemakers let trade buyers from around the world taste their newest vintages and the vins clairs from the recent harvest. This time of year be a little dangerous for the amateur imbiber—it's Champagne Overload and I have been known to get myself into a little too much trouble!

SECRET CODES ON A WINE LABEL: YES, YOU CAN BE TOM HANKS AND BREAK CODES TOO!

On a wine label, you will notice the little abbreviations "RM," "NM," or "RC." While these are not prominently displayed, they indicate (respectively) whether a wine is made by a winemaker who only bottles estate fruit, a house who purchases grapes from growers and may or may not own its own vineyards, or a group of winemakers who grow grapes and produce wines under a label that comes out of a group effort.

RM

Growers and *Vignerons* aka RM (Relcoltant Minipulant)
These are landowners who grow grapes and produce their wines from solely those grapes.

NM

Maisons aka Houses aka NM (Negociant Minipulant)
Often (but not always), these brands purchase a portion of their grapes from growers to produce their wines.

RC

Cooperatives aka RC (Recolcant Cooperative)
A winemaker or wine that grows grapes and then sends the grapes to a cooperative for wine pressing and production. In turn, they are given completed bottles of wine that they put under their own label or a collective's label.

GOOD CHAMPAGNE
COSTS GOOD MONEY,
BUT SOMETIMES THAT
SCARES PEOPLE AWAY
FROM TRYING SOME
REALLY GREAT STUFF.
SO TO MAKE IT LESS
SCARY, I AM GOING TO
RATE EACH BOTTLE WITH
HOW MANY PIZZAS IT
WOULD COST. (BECAUSE
YOU KNOW I LOVE PIZZA.)
GUESSTIMATING
$25 PER PIZZA.

THE OG ORIGINALS NOW LEADING THE CHARGE

These are the winemakers at the fore-front of the Grower Champagne "movement." I air-quotes movement because the tides were turning long before the wines ever got much recognition. They were first to the US market and almost all of them make wine for multi-genera-tional wineries. The vineyards have been passed down through the family and the current wine-makers really took it upon themselves to question why and how their families had made Cham-pagne before them. Some continue the traditions but with a more thoughtful approach, others have changed style, technique, and practices. Respect and obsession has only grown for these wines, making them some of the most sought after in the world.

Pierre Péters
Rodolphe Péters
Les Chétillons
Blanc de Blanc: Chardonnay
Les Mesnil sur Oger
Coffee ice cream

René Geoffroy
Jean-Baptiste Geoffroy
Blanc de Rosé
Blend: Pinot Noir + Chardonnay
Aÿ
Strawberry rhubarb pie
🥂🥂🥂🥂🥂

Georges Laval
Vincent Laval
Premier Cru Brut Nature Cumières
Blend: Pinot Noir + Chardonnay +
Pinot Meunier
Cumières
Powdered raspberry candy
🥂🥂 1/2

Pascal Doquet
Pascal Doquet
Arpege
Blanc de Blanc: 100% Chardonnay
Vertus
Green apple galette
🥂🥂

Gaston Chiquet
Antoine, Nicolas, and Marion Chiquet
Tradition Premier Cru
Blend: Pinot Meunier + Chardonnay
+ Pinot Noir
Dizy
Quince jam
🥂🥂 1/2

Gimmonet
Didier Gimonnet
Special Club 2012
Blanc de Blanc
Cuis
Flat white coffee

Egly-Ouriet
Francis Egly
Vieilles Vignes de Vrigny
Blanc de Noir: 100% Pinot Meunier
Ambonnay
Dried Plums
🥂 1/2

Benoît Lahaye
Benoît Lahaye
Rosé de Maceration
Blanc de Noir: Pinot Noir
Bouzy
Chocolate covered cherries
🥂🥂🥂

Vazart Coquart
Jean-Pierre Vazart
Special Club 2010
Blanc de Blanc
Chouilly
Honeycomb
🥂🥂🥂🥂

MY CHAMPAGNE DAD...
AND THE MOMENT I KNEW
IT WOULD ALL BE OKAY

At twenty-three years old, I went to Champagne for the first time. I barely looked a day over twenty, and not to hammer home my innocence and naivety, but I brought my mother along for my first adventure. Picture the scenario and then ask yourself, would you have taken me seriously as a Champagne buyer? Oh, also, I kinda speak French, but definitely don't speak French well.

So when we knocked on the door of Jean Paul Hebrart, he was surprised. The appointment he thought he had with an important buyer from Chicago ended up being an appointment with me and my Queens-born, no-bullshit, Jewish mama. (I was then working for Pops for Champagne and the person who booked my appointment had told a little white lie. See, fake it.)

I could sense his confusion, or maybe disappointment (or maybe he's just French, so inherently skeptical). But that afternoon, one of the most important relationships of my career blossomed.

I like to say that the Champenoise are the Midwesterners of France. They are generous, gracious, family oriented, and have values deeply rooted in tradition. Not to mention they will be real nice to your face and talk a lot of smack behind your back. It's cool Midwest. I've learned how to navigate you, wink.

Jean Paul is the prime example of the quintessential Champenois. In our broken half-English, half-French conversation, it didn't take more than moments for us to begin talking about generations of family influence and the desire for progress while maintaining tradition. We walked his vineyards together and tasted his vin clair and fresh bottle disgorgements that afternoon. He jokingly said I could come take over the family business. His son was into tennis and he wasn't sure what the future held.

I dubbed Jean Paul my "Champagne Dad." He was the person who sponsored my invitation to Les Prentemps de Champagne the year following our visit. It's a big honor to be invited by Les Artisans, a democratic group of winemakers who discuss philosophy and production techniques. It felt like a sort of coming out, a NYC debutante in Champagne. I remember when Jean Paul introduced me to Laurent Champs from Vilmart et Cie, whom I had only dreamed of meeting, and I felt his pride in our friendship. I still regularly visit him and hold his wines as the benchmark of quality and deliciousness.

JP had never been to NYC, and during visits to him over the years I would push the subject. In 2018, he stepped into Air's for the first time. You would have thought Prince was there. I died.

THE NEW GEN

Dhondt-Grellet
Adrien Dhondt
Cramant 100% from the Grand Cru Village
Blanc de Blanc: 100% Chardonnay
Flavigny
Iced Coffee with Cream
🍾🍾1/2

Domaine Nowack
Flavien Nowack
La Fontinette
Blanc de Noir: 100% Pinot Meunier
Vandières
Fuji apple
🍾🍾1/2

Guillaume Selosse
Guillaume Selosse
Largillier
Blanc de Noir: 100% Pinot Noir
Côte des Bar
Crunch Bar of flowers and sherry
🍾 x 16

Pierre Gerbais
Aurélien Gerbais
L'Originale
Blanc de Blanc: 100% Pinot Blanc
Celles-sur-Ource
Fresh chevre
🍾🍾1/2

Here's a curated selection of the winemakers making waves, young guys pushing the limits of Champagne with a deep understanding of terroir. Each of these winemakers work a portion of their family's land, which has been passed down through generations. Some of them didn't think they would become *vignerons* and yet it was their calling. Others knew becoming a winemaker was always in their blood.

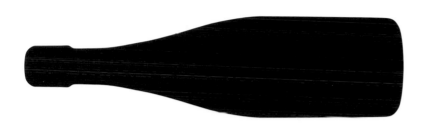

Suenen
Aurelien Suenen
C+C
Blanc de Blanc: 100% Chardonnay
Cramant
Honeysuckle
🥂🥂

Doyard
Oeil de Perdrix
Pedrix Style: Chardonnay + Pinot Noir
Vertus
Potpourri
🥂🥂🥂

Mouzon Leroux
Sébastien Mouzon
L'Atavique
Blended Pinot Noir + Chardonnay
Verzy
Fresh cherries
🥂🥂

JM Sélèque
Jean-Marc Sélèque
Solessence Rosé
Blended saignée + still red wine: Pinot Noir + Chardonnay + Pinot Meunier
Pierry
Raspberry tart
🥂 1/2

THE
UNTOUCHABLES

SELOSSE

Two Champagnes changed my life.

One happened when I was working in Chicago for Chef Grant Achetz's The Office under The Aviary. The Office is the mecca to spirits, only offering the very best and rare. At this time, I was a bona fide novice to Champagne, although I was pretty firm on the notion that I fucking loved it.

One night a woman came in and ordered a bottle of Jacques Selosse Substance. I was relatively clueless on this wine, but I knew it was special: it was the most expensive Champagne on the list and it wasn't even vintage.

It is and was a SOLERA, which is a technique of creating a consistent, complex, and generally old NV wine that is a mixture of many different vintages.

Remember when we talked about reserves and how a winemaker is mandated to keep some juice from every year, just in case? Some producers take this to an extreme and put more than that percentage into one large barrel or tank. Every year they add to it, and most years they extract from it to create new wine. This creates a homogenous relationship between young and old, with the new reserves taking on the characteristics of the old wine.

Tangent: It's like when my dad wouldn't let me listen to the top-forty radio station as a kid and raised me exclusively on soul and classic rock, so by the time I was ten years old, I was singing Aretha Franklin and Tom Petty.

These Soleras—sometimes called Perpetual Reserves (depending on how often the wine is added and extracted)—can range from fresh with complexity to dense and chewy.

Selosse Substance finds a hybrid between both. Started in 1986, and made from all Chardonnay from the Grand Cru village of Avize, this wine is butterscotch and honey and toasted almonds and apple pie and everything great in the world in one bottle. Little did I know it was one of the most sought-after Champagnes, and this woman—bless her heart—took one sip and said,

"I think this is off. There is something wrong with it."

Completely shocked, and under the assumption the customer was always right, I took the wine back to my General Manager and asked him to taste it. He took a sip, his eyes did that thing where they popped out of his head like a cartoon character, and he handed the glass to me to try.

Sometimes I still can't understand how a wine can taste like a velvet blanket being pulled down your body on top of a bearskin rug in front of a fireplace in a cabin in the snow-drifted woods of New Hampshire. That wine was seductive and electric and rich and powerful—and that woman was an idiot.

She asked to see the wine list again and ordered something else. And my GM and I got to drink the Selosse Substance.

Anselm Selosse is UNTOUCHABLE because he's just the best at the style he creates. He works mainly with Grand Cru Chardonnay except for a small amount of Pinot Noir that goes into a single parcel, single village, single varietal wine (say that three times fast). These wines are called the Lieux Dit Series.

Anselm is the godfather of Burgundy-style Champagne—essentially terroir-focused wines—from all angles: an intense focus on the soil, farming practices, sorting and pressing based on village and parcel, fermentation in wood, extended aging, and the idea that wine made with so much thoughtfulness and care should not be dosed heavily with excess sugars.

He probably wasn't the first to implement these practices, but the sum of these methods in the early 1980s was a game changer for the region of Champagne. He has since influenced countless winemakers, many of whom I will highlight, and his son Guillaume is now at the helm, continuing the family tradition as well as adding to it with his own wines.

Champagne Krug

The other life-changing Champagne also happened when I was working at The Office. Chef was entertaining one late night. He was a fan of Krug Champagne, and nothing is more iconic than that gold-foiled bottle. When the night was over, there was some left in a bottle, enough to taste. I knew about Krug but had never tasted it, and I had a question: "What's going on here?"

The thing is, I didn't really get it. When I sipped the leftover Krug, I noted a nice acidity and freshness, but I was simply unaware how this was the best Grand Mark Champagne or Maison wine on the market. I was not particularly wowed on that first sip to drop a hot take. And it took me another six years before I tasted Krug again, with a more developed palate so I could pick up on its nuance and structure.

The history of Krug is a long one, but the story basically goes that in 1843, Joseph Krug had this idea that terroir (see—a common theme) would play a major role in creating truly exceptional Champagne. He directed everything to be vinified separately, according to village and plot, and that the wine be blended to as many vintages as possible and aged on the lees in the cellar for as long as possible. They would use Pinot Noir, Meunier, and Chardonnay to create a Prestige House Cuvée, and even though these wines would be very old by the time they were released, they were still going to be NVs.

Since the beginning of Champagne, the goal has been both lengthy aging and a blend of multiple vintages. When you think of time as money, you can understand how why these wines have gained the reputation for excellence as well as luxury.

It still always amazes me, no matter the setting—say, a natural wine bar where people are romanticizing the ideas of low intervention and biodynamic practices—and everyone's glass goes up if the Krug comes out. It's a secret weapon wine, and on many occasions after a big tasting of Champagne, a novice drinker will pull me aside and say, "They were all amazing, but I think I like the Krug."

A few years ago, I had the pleasure of befriending Olivier Krug, of the Sixth Generation of the House of Krug. Olivier and I were seated next to each other at a lunch for the launch of the 2004 Krug Vintage, a wine that is aged ten years on the lees until released. We got to talking and someone introduced me and mentioned my Japanese record bar in New York City, Tokyo Record Bar, that had just opened weeks before. Olivier, if he hadn't gone into the business of Champagne, would have dreamed of going into the music industry and was a diehard fan of the alternative-rock band the Pixies as well as avant-garde gothic-rock artist Nico. Just my luck! Halfway through our lunch and the deep dive into our musical tastes, a cake came out and the whole room began to sing "Happy Birthday." The cake was dropped smack in front of us, and it turns out that my dining companion was actually the birthday boy. Over blown-out candles, Olivier promised to come DJ at my little hole in the wall in the fall, and months later I got to DJ alongside him at Tokyo Record Bar.

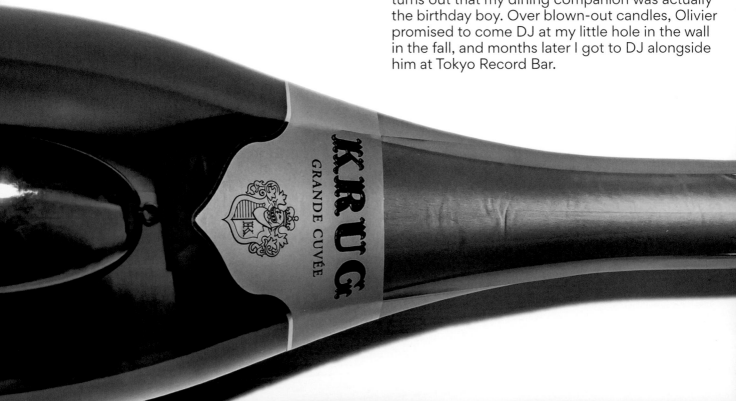

OLIVIER KRUG'S PLAYLIST
FOR TOKYO RECORD BAR NOV. 17TH, 2017

Krug Grande Cuvée 164th Édition: FATS DOMINO: "Blueberry Hill"
(tribute to the founder of Rock and Roll, who passed away last week)

Krug 2004: NOUVELLE VAGUE: "Love Will Tear Us Apart" (which both
Ariel and I found matching the luminous freshness, elegance and depth,
as well as an immensely original New Wave piece)

AND

VELVET UNDERGROUND: "I'll Be Your Mirror" (circumstances of the
year mirrored by Cuvée n'2. By the most influential band ever, in NY's
Warhol's factory, not far from the Bar)

Krug Rosé: DAVID BOWIE: "Rebel Rebel" (speaks for itself)

Krug Grande Cuvée 160th Édition:
LOU REED: "Walk on the Wild Side"

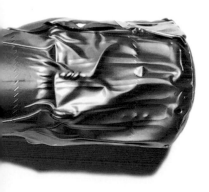

VIGNERONS

THE WINEMAKERS' WINEMAKERS

Vilmart et Cie
Laurent Champs
Grand Cellier
Blended: Chardonnay + Pinot Noir
Rilly-la-Montagne
Candied ginger
🍕🍕

Ulysse Collin
Olivier Collin
Les Perriades
Blanc de Blanc: 100% Chardonnay
Congy
Hazelnut pie
🍕🍕

Jérôme Prévost —
Champagne La Closerie
Jérôme Prévost
Les Béguines Extra Brut
Blanc de Noir: 100% Pinot Meunier
Gueux
Blackberry bramble
🍕🍕🍕

Roses de Jeanne
Cédric Bouchard
Les Ursules
Blanc de Noir: 100% Pinot Noir
Celles-sur-Ource
Toasted cashews
🍕🍕🍕

Eric Rodez
Eric Rodez
Rosé
Blended Rosé: Chardonnay + Pinot Noir
Ambonnay
Roasted raspberries
🍕1/2

These are serious winemakers. They have been in the game long enough to produce some of the most exciting yet consistent wines that people show off on social media, save for special occasions, and age in cellars. These wines are often made in small production, and definitely give credibility to the drinker if named-dropped. And they are as much about the cellar as the vineyard—a lot of the magic happens after the grapes are harvested.

Agrapart & Fils
Pascal Agrapart
Mineral
Blanc de Blanc: 100% Chardonnay
Avize
Apple pie
🥂 1/2

R. Pouillon
Fabrice Pouillon
Les Valnons
Blanc de Blanc
Aÿ
Chai Tea
🥂🥂 1/2

Chartogne-Taillet
Alexandre Chartogne
Orizeaux
Blanc de Noir: 100% Pinot Noir
Merfy
Spicy French vanilla
🥂🥂🥂

Emmanuel Brochet
Emmanuel Brochet
Mont Benoît Lieu-Dit
Blend: Chardonnay + Pinot Noir+ Pinot Meunier
Villers-aux- Nœuds
Sweet cream
🥂🥂

Savart
Frederic Savart
L'Ouverture
Blanc de Noir: 100% Pinot Noir
Écueil
Blueberry yoghurt
🥂 1/2

THE WILD MAN & THE LEGEND

Rarely, you get the pleasure of meeting someone with immense character. I am lucky that I have met two in my more than a decade of experience in the industry: Fabrice Gass and Marie Noelle Ledru, who are winemakers' winemakers. Respected by their peers, these two have very different stories but I consider them to be outstanding in their field—these two do it all, vineyard to bottle. The year 2017 was Marie Noelle's last vintage, and Fabrice only makes a small amount of wine so these can be hard to come by. If you find these unicorns, cherish them.

WILD MAN
Alexandre Filaine

Fabrice Gass spent the majority of his professional career as Chef de Cave at Bollinger and learned his trade from the old guard—his grandparents. He now makes his own Champagne in a back shed outside his house and produces about five thousand bottles. When I met Fabrice, he was always with his two best friends, Janette and X.

He practices *lutte raisonnée*, a method that is a happy medium between conventional techniques and organic farming. Champagne has a very difficult climate, and it's not so simple for someone to say, "I want to be exactly xyz." It's also important to note that in a large village, there will be hundreds of wine growers that own different plots adjacent to one another. All that is to say if you are following biodynamic or organic principles, that doesn't mean your neighbor is as well.

Alexandre Filaine
Fabrice Gass
DMY
Blended: Pinot Noir + Chardonnay + Pinot Meunier
Damery
Hazelnut torte
🥂🥂🥂🥂

THE LEGEND
Marie Noelle Ledru

My friend Craig Perman had recommended a bottle of one of Marie's wines to me. He has a lovely shop in Chicago called Permen's Wines. It was in early days in my career and Perman had access to wines I had never seen, heard of, or tasted. It was a bottle of Rosé, which is basically a unicorn now. It was simply divine.

The thing to understand is, when a wine is incredible and you know it's incredible, it's probably going to be hard to get. SO STOCKPILE NOW, FRIENDS.

Marie Noelle Ledru was like the cronut in its early days, unavailable seemingly overnight. Marie had made her last vintage in 2017 and it was rumored she would probably not be taking many visitors in the future. So when I got the opportunity to visit her in 2018, it was a dream come true. Then there was a big party in Reims the night before the visit, and I had too good of a time. I ended up tripping over my feet on a cobblestone street and smashed my face on the sidewalk. Needless to say, for my visit, I had a solid gash over my right eye and a bruised face. Oh, and definitely a concussion. And our appointment was at ten o'clock in the morning.

As she pulled bottles out of the cellar and hand disgorged them, I felt as though I was in a dream. My head was in the clouds, and Marie seemed to have an angel's halo around her. It was almost like the pain mixed with the wine created a sensory overload and I was in a waking dream state, almost euphoric. She gave me ice for my face, and head cheese because she's mad French. I should have felt mortified, but I didn't, because she gave me a look as if she knew all too well what Champagne could do to a girl. I don't recommend a concussion for winetasting but I gotta say, that day was one I'll never forget, brain function be damned.

Marie-Noëlle Ledru
Brut Nature
Blanc de Noir: 100% Pinot Noir
Ambonnay
Unripe plums
It's hard to rate the price on these wines now.
They were once about two pizzas but it's
anyone's bet how expensive they've become.
3🍕–6🍕

BROTHER-BROTHER/ BROTHER-BROTHER-SISTER SITUATIONS

These wines are a family affair. One year, when the Air's Champagne team took a trip to Champagne, we entered a tasting room where every winery presenting had three generations of cuties making the wines. Amanda, our fabuloso employee said, "What is this brother brother daddy situation?" And, well, the phrase stuck. We have also evolved this signature to include mommies and sisters. Many of these dynamic duos or trios have taken over the business from their parents and share the responsibilities of winemaking. Often one family member spends their time in the vineyards while the other will be more focused on the cellar.

Huré Frères
Huré Hermanos: Pierre and François
L'Invitation
Blend with Solera dating to 1982
Ludes
Blackberry Bramble
🍾 1/2

Bérêche et Fils
Bérêche Brothers: Raphaël and Vincent
Rive Gauche
Blanc de Noir: 100% Pinot Mounier
Ludes
Black pepper butter
🍾🍾🍾🍾

Pierre Paillard
Paillard Bros: Antoine & Quenten
Les Maillerettes
Blanc de Noir: 100% Pinot Noir
Bouzy
Black cherry jam
🍾🍾🍾

Tarlant
Tarlant Takeover: Mélanie & Benoît
BAM Non-Dosage
Blend: Pinot Blanc, Arbane & Petit Meslier
Oeuilly
Jasmine flowers
🍾🍾🍾🍾🍾

THE BIODYNAMICS AND ORGANICS

Marguet
Benoit Marguet
Ambonnay
*Biodynamic & Demeter-Certified
Blend: Pinot Noir + Chardonnay
Ambonnay
Tarte framboise
🍾🍾🍾🍾🍾

Jacques Lassaigne
Emmanuel Lassaigne
Vignes de Montgueux
*Organic
Blanc de Blanc: 100% Chardonnay
Montgueux
Farmhouse apple cider
🍾1/2

Vouette et Sorbée
Bertrand Gautherot
Textures
*Biodynamic Certified + Organic+ Sustainable
Blanc de Blanc: 100% Pinot Blanc
Côte des Bars
Salted hazelnuts
🍾🍾🍾🍾🍾

These winemakers have a strong sense of place as well as philosophy. Some biodynamic winemakers are fully certified, while others practice without being certified. But they all hold themselves to a high standard using techniques guided by biodynamic principles for their terroir.

Charles Dufour
Charles Dufour
Bulles de Comptoir Assemblage #7
*Organic
Blend: Pinot Noir, Chardonnay, and Pinot Blanc
Landreville
White currants
🍕🍕

Laherte Frères
Aurelien
Ultradition
*Practicing Organic & Biodynamic
Pinot Meunier, Chardonnay, and Pinot Noir
Chavot
Lemon zest
🍕 1/2

Leclerc Briant
Hervé Jestin
Brut Reserve
*Practicing Organic & Biodynamic
Blend: Pinot Noir, Chardonnay, Pinot Meunier
Épernay
Dark chocolate-covered almonds
🍕🍕

MEUNIER TAKE OVER

There has been an amazing selection of 100 percent Pinot Meunier wines coming to market, and I believe there are many more to come. As we discussed earlier, these wines used to be thought of as second-rate—not great for ageability due to the grape's ease of growing and large yields, and not incredibly dynamic. WRONG! Meunier is the Evel Knievel, Kerri Strugg, Rocky Balboa of Champagne.

Christophe Mignon
Christophe Mignon
Brut Nature
Festigny
Fresh cracked pepper
🍾🍾 1/2

Moussé Fils
Cédric Moussé
Les Vignes de Mon Village
Cuisles
Fuji apple
🍾🍾

Aurelien Lurquin
Aurelien Lurquin
Les Crayeres du Levant
Romery
Fresh brioche with salted butter
🍾🍾🍾🍾

BABES 'N' BUBBLES

The women of Champagne have a bit of a bad reputation, mostly because a lot of their husbands have ended up dead. The most famous is the Grand Dame: the Widow Cliquot, or the "Riddling Widow." The story goes like this: After her husband dies of typhoid fever, Barbe-Nicole Ponsardin-Cliquot, a young woman of twenty-six, is left with a company involved in wool, banking, and Champagne production. She decides that Champagne will become her family business and eventually is credited with gigantic strides in the industry: disgorgement of yeast from a Champagne bottle (yeah, a babe invented this), sabering, and Rosé. Not a bad legacy.

Fun fact: The yellow labels that bear her wines translate as Widow (Veuve) Cliquot.

Plenty of women in wine history were widowed and had to manage the vineyards and tend to the cellars, but many took over their families' businesses, bought property of their own, and grew up in the vineyards knowing that they would be *vignerons*. With Barbe-Nicole's legacy as one of the most influential business owners in all of Champagne, it's unsurprising that so many women have come to create their own legacy in the region.

Nathalie Falmet
Nathalie Falmet
Extra Brut
Blend: Pinot Noir + Chardonnay
Côte des Bar
Rose petals
🥂🥂

Marie Courtin
Dominique Moreau
Presence
Blanc de Blanc: Chardonnay +
Pinot Blanc
Polisot
Fresh cut white flowers
🥂🥂 1/2

H. Billiot Fils
Laetitia Billiot
Brut Rosé
Blend: Pinot Noir + Chardonnay
Ambonnay
Raspberry Tangerine
🥂 1/2

Henriet-Bazin
Marie-Noelle Bazin
Blanc de Noir Grand Cru
Blanc de Noir: 100% Pinot Noir
Villers-Marmery
Chocolate covered cherries
🥂 1/2

Françoise Bedel
Françoise Bedel
Dis, Vin Secret
Blend: Pinot Meunier + Chardonnay
Crouttes-sur-Marne
Salted caramel
🥂🥂

Corbon:
Humble brag, it's my
birth year! I'm not a
great vintage, and
this is one of the only
cellars that produced
it AND still has it
kicking around.

It was the first time
I ever tasted my
birth year from
Champagne, and the
wine tasted like an
antipasta salad.

J. Lassalle
Angéline Templier
Cuvée Angeline Premier Cru Vintage
Blend: Pinot Noir + Chardonnay
Chigny-les-Roses
Strawberry rhubarb pie
🥂🥂🥂🥂

Corbon
Agnès Corbon
Vintage 1987
Blanc de Blanc: 100% Chardonnay
Avize
🥂🥂🥂🥂

VINTAGES

We live in a world where if we want a tomato or a banana, we can have it all year long and (if you live in a city like NYC) any time of the day or night. In our day-to-day life, we don't often think about how a season's being a bit colder, rainier, hotter, muggier, drier, or more humid than usual can impact crops. But in Champagne, one bad frost can mean a winemaker will lose an entire harvest. A year can be unseasonably warm, and all the wines taste baked or burned. Then there are some seasons that seem perfect—cold when needed and hot at the right time—yet they produce good but not great Champagnes, and there are other years, when disaster strikes, that produce ethereal, magnificent and complex wines. Vintage wines are rare because the most exceptional ones come out of exceptional, sometimes supernatural, conditions, and it's often Quality over Quantity.

It's not always the case that "small quantities" mean "exceptional," but often vintage wines use just the best grapes to produce in smaller amounts. And once in a while there are excellent vintages that provide you with quality and quantity.

Here are what the critics say are the best vintages of the twentieth and twenty-first century. I think everything comes down to taste. There is much variation in vintages, and there are many producers that make incredible wines in less than favorable years.

CRITICALLY ACCLAIMED VINTAGES AND AN IN-DEPTH FOCUS ON THE TWENTY-FIRST CENTURY

1928, 1929, 1937, 1945, 1947, 1949, 1953, 1959, 1961, 1964, 1971, 1973, 1979, 1985, 1988, 1990, 1995, 1996, 1998, 2002, 2004, 2008, 2012, 2015

PS: The oldest Champagne I have tasted is from the late 1960s, so I can't speak from personal experience about wines from the 1920s through most of the 1960s.

It's important to look at what's happening in the twenty-first century in a little more detail. With climate change, the seasons are shifting, which is changing the many ways winemakers work in their vineyards. For a vintage wine to get to your table, it takes roughly four years (three years minimum), so let's start with what is actually available to you on the market, starting in 2016.

2016

Right around the time the grapevines started to flower (earlier than they traditionally did, due to the climate shift), there was a huge sweep of frost and hail that wrecked the vineyards. Unfortunately, the harvest was worse off in the southern part of the region, and Pinot Noir ended up performing better than Chardonnay in this vintage.

2015

This year was exceptionally dry with not a lot of rainfall. Warm days with plenty of sun led to a high ripeness during the harvest season. (In Champagne, it's okay for the temperatures to be warm, even hot—as long as the vineyards don't get so hot that the grapes begin to bake or the acidity disappears due to a sugar takeover.) This vintage is being called exceptional, and it will be quite ripe. Pinot Noir is the grape to keep your eye on.

2014

I am loving 2014. The end of summer suffered some rain and was all-around damp, which usually has the potential to dilute density in the grapes. But during September and harvest, the temperatures were moderate—if not a bit warm—which helped to ripen them. I find the grapes to have a coolness and a slightly softer element to them. They feel a little spicy and light and drink well right out of the glass.

2013

Again, this isn't a heralded vintage, but I love it for its high acidity. This season started cold and was particularly long due to a late flowering and a late harvest. Some crazy hail over the summer damaged vineyards. When I tasted the '13 vin clair, I kept thinking how this vintage felt like a very mysterious woman—like you couldn't tell if she was crazy or magical. Maybe both. Most wines are on the lean side, with high acid and zest.

2012

Major frost and hail in the beginning of the season substantially lowered the quantity. But overall excellent conditions led to grapes' having an amazing balance of acidity and maturity. This vintage has a crazy density to it. It is balanced, and yet part of me doesn't feel a crazy spark. Don't get me wrong—the wines are delicious and opulent, but this is a safe vintage. It's lacking some je ne sais quois that would really make it dynamic.

2011

All the critics called this vintage too young. When it first came to market, it was green and bitter and herbal and minty. It wasn't pleasing, for sure. It got a bad rep even though the growing season didn't necessarily mean it was going to be a bad vintage. The season was warm early on, with not a lot of rain, but then flipped and became cool and wet during the later months of the summer. Near the end of the season, the clouds parted for a bit, but then the rain picked back up during harvest. I definitely was an early nose-turn-upper to this vintage, but over time I have revisited these wines repeatedly. Most of those initial characteristics have either blown away or are almost undetectable now. It's actually a lovely vintage, still holding on to some herbal notes, but almost all the bitterness is gone. This vintage is a great deal, because no one bought them and they are drinking well now and will continue to! (I always say, if everyone in Champagne chooses to make a vintage during a particular year, you have to trust that there is something they saw in it.)

2010

This was not a great season. There was tons of rain, with rot and mildew developing as a result. It was difficult to have good, consistent quality. The vintage is not bad, but it's just not special, and there wasn't a lot produced.

2009

This vintage is an example of really good conditions. It was a warm season, and not out of the ordinary for rain or heat. The wines are rich and supple and hedge more on the fruit than acidity end.

2008

I fucking love '08! I have loved it since the moment I tasted it. It's a beautiful bouquet of fruit, ripe but not too rich. I love it for Pinot Noir specifically. Because the wines were luscious out of the gate, it was under-rated. Critics tend to think there needs to be a ton of tension and complexity for a vintage to be excellent, but sometimes delicious is just excellent and that's how I feel about these wines, damn it! There were issues of some rot and mildew in the beginning due to high concentrations of rain, but the summer warmed up and August and September were dry.

2007

I keep talking about flowering—when the vines burst open with flowers for the first time each year. This happens in the early spring when soil temperatures warm. This vintage is a perfect example of an early flowering immediately followed by humidity, warmth, and rain, leading to a fine harvest but nothing spectacular. This year is known for Chardonnay.

2006

There is a strong freshness and minerality to 2006, even though the harvest was thought to be—to quote Jancis Robinson—"dank." I like to think of '06, '07, and '08 along a spectrum, in which 2006 is on the lighter end and the vintages grow richer and fuller, with less acidity and more fruit, by 2008.

2005

This vintage packs the heat, but not the finesse. It was an all-around temperamental year with a turnaround harvest that created ripeness in the grapes. If you like richness and a lot of soft baked qualities in your Champagne, this could be the year for you!

2004

This is one of my favorite vintages. When it first came to market, everyone was calling it young and tight. It did show a lot of acidity up front, but there was a honeyed expression that I immediately fell in love with. It was a "quality and quantity" wine so the pricing was affordable, and I poured them from a bunch of different producers in my restaurants forever. Then a few years after they were released, their character came out in full force! They became Winnie the Pooh, scooping out ripe, rich honey from a pot. I also love this vintage because it shows evolution unlike any other. These wines drink incredibly animalistic now: their character has changed immensely, turning deep, dark, and seductive. They are still affordable but they get picked up fast, so unfortunately this amazing vintage is hard to find. If you can find them, buy them!

2003

This vintage was Martha Reeves and the Vandellas—a heatwave! Burnt and hot. If you like big toasty wines, these might be for you.

2002

A perfect vintage, optimal on all fronts. The season was cold up to flowering, warm during the spring, hot during summer with just the right amount of water, and dry during harvest. It's thought of as being the classic vintage of the twenty-first century. It's def delicious.

2001

This vintage was a bust. No one made wine during this season—it was such a bad harvest with lots of rain and rot.

2000

This season started off the new century with non-ideal conditions, but, by the end of the harvest, the season was dry and warm. These wines follow 1999, which people claim is a great vintage, though I am not a huge fan of the '99s. That vintage feels a little dirty and dusty to me, while 2000 feels a more balanced option. These wines are fine, nice, even reasonable for their age.

SALON!

Salon is a special kind of house, mainly because of its very small production. It is an entire maison based around one grape (Chardonnay), one place (Les Mesi), and one vintage. As of 2019, only thirty-eight vintages have been released since 1921. In the years they deem the vintage of insufficient quality for the house, they sell the grapes to their sister house, Delamotte. In the most bountiful of years, the greatest amount of wines they will produce is sixty thousand bottles.

On my first visit to Champagne, I took my mom to Salon. I have since been back with old friends, my father, and business partners, but on that very first visit, it felt as though we were stepping into a futuristic spaceship. The very old cellar had just undergone a transformation for the tasting room—next to old brick and bottles was a *Jetsons*-esque white-and-cream circle bar that felt as if Rosie was going to pop up from behind it and serve me.

That day, my mother declared that Salon was her favorite. I wasn't surprised—the woman had expensive taste. We always celebrated the holidays, her birthdays, and special occasions with Salon when I could get my hands on it.

I sprinkled Mom's ashes in the vineyards of Le Mesnil on Sunday, April 22, 2018, at 5:59 pm. On the drive from Epernay with my friend Adrien Dhondt, I listened to Stevie Wonder "Saturn," and, as if by magic, the next song to come on was Stevie's "If It's Magic."

Adrien commented on the time of day: the sun was setting and it was that perfect moment of twilight. We hadn't planned to go out to the vineyards at that time, but somehow it happened that way. Mom's favorite time of day was sunset.

We drove up to the top of Les Mesnil, and I found a nice shady bramble that overlooked town. As I pulled out the ziplocked bag of ashes to sprinkle, a bumblebee appeared. I laughed with tears in my eyes, knowing it was my mother—such a busybody, a Jewish mom who's always gotta know what's going on. When I got up the courage to open the bag, the bells of the church rang. The entire town filled with sound. It was a moment of pure magic. It was six o'clock. The sun was setting. My Mom, the bee, was there with me.

MAISONS
I LOVE

Gosset
Celebris
Blend: Pinot Noir + Chardonnay
Épernay
Blackberry cream
🥂🥂🥂🥂🥂

Jacquesson
737 Dégorgement Tardif
Blend: Pinot Noir + Chardonnay
Dizy
Sandalwood
🥂 x 10

Pol Roger
Winston Churchill 2002
Blend: Pinot Noir + Chardonnay
Épernay
Iced Latte
🥂 x 10

I am all about equal opportunity and you cannot fully grasp grower Champagne if you don't taste foundational and historical Maison wines. For the money and the quality these are some of my absolute favorites. Incredible winemaking happens here with generational relationships with farmers who grow their grapes.

Bollinger
R.D. Extra Brut
(Note "R.D." refers to récemment dégorgé, which means "disgorged late," or "extended aging." Another term for this is dégorgement tardif.)
Blend: Pinot Noir + Chardonnay
Aÿ
Ferrero Rocher
🥂 x 26

Philiponnat
Clos de Goisses
Blend: Pinot Noir + Chardonnay
Mareuil-sur-Ay
🥂 x 8

Henroit
Cuvée des Enchanteleurs
Blend: Pinot Noir + Chardonnay
Reims
Buttered popcorn
🥂 x 7

Champagne Charlie
Brut
Blended
🐟 x 30

CHARLES HEIDSIECK

CHARLES HEIDSIECK

Charles Heidsieck is one of the oldest operating maisons that has access to les Crayères—old Roman cellars that date back to the third century—and only one of five Champagne houses that has this access. This thirty-meter-deep underground labyrinth cellar, dug out of chalk, has the ideal temperature for aging wine. The les Crayères investment made it possible for the house to achieve a style of Champagne that had more to do with long-term ageing than terroir and vineyard ownership. The house purchased the cellars in 1867, and since then their non-vintage cuvée has been made up of 50 percent reserve wines that can lie dormant in the cellars for up to forty years.

Side Note: I was lucky enough to pull this bottle directly from the cellar, otherwise known as the Oenotheque, and drink it freshly disgorged.

CHAMPAGNE CHARLIE

The Maison Charles Heidsieck has a storied history, like many of the old houses, but one of my favorite things about Champagne brands is that they always have one that they are really proud of. Every time I would hear the origin story of Charles Heidsieck, it felt ripe for film—so I decided to write its treatment. Technically there was a movie made in 1989, but I've really spiced it up, giving it a Champagne overhaul. Any producers out there—feel free to reach out!

An Arcecool Production
Charles Heidsieck: played by a Leo DiCaprio type

Opening Credits

The United States, Five Years before the Civil War

Known as Champagne Charlie, Charles H. arrived in Boston in 1852, the first head of a Champagne house to visit America.

We see him exit out of a carriage on a cobbled stone street.

SETTING: NEW YORK CITY.
A closeup as he lifts his head and removes his top hat, revealing a young man with a soft twinkle in his eyes.

He has a Great Gatsby je ne sais quois mixed with the playfulness of Jack in Titanic and the cockiness of a *Bonfires of the Vanities* trader.

Charles hires himself a wine agent and over the course of five years and a few montages we watch him become the number-one Champagne producer in the United States.
He spends his time running around town with girls and wine doing deals.
In the early hours of the morning he writes letters to his wife, two kids, and a dog.

The Wife: A real Jennifer Biel type.

FIVE YEARS LATER
With the Civil War looming, Charles has unpaid debts.

The country is at odds (sound familiar?) and Charlie's wine agent flees NYC and leaves him broke.

CUT TO NEW SCENE
Charlie dons an amazing pair of cowboy boots, trades in his tux for a cargo duster, and heads to New Orleans to try and collect his debt from merchants.
Closeup on his double-breasted western rifle attached to his belt and a horse named Jacob as he rides into town.
Wide shot of wisteria and a wrought-iron-clad buildings on either side of him.

Charlie:
I'm here to collect from you merchants!

Merchants:
We're all broke, Charlie, but we'll trade our debts for cotton!

Charlie:
Really? Ugh, fine, I'll take it.

CUT TO NEW SCENE
Charlie is at the dock on a foggy, wet night watching his cargo of cotton ship off to France.
The moonlight streams through ominous clouds, and you can smell war in the air.
Union soldiers approach in the distance.
An explosion! (Note to self: talk to JJ Abrams about pyrotechnics.)

BACK TO . . .
Union soldiers apprehend Charlie, arrest him, and charge him with spying.
He is jailed . . . gasp!

FIVE MONTHS LATER
A *Revenant*-esque Charles is on the edge of death.
Cinematic note: We want to see a lot of unshaved face, some crusty snot, and a lot of ragged clothing plus lots of dusty light streaming in through the jail's barred windows.

A parchment letter arrives at the jail. It reads:
The North has won, Lincoln has pardoned Heidsieck, and he should be returned to France at once!

TRANSITION TO
Back in Champagne, Charlie steps out of a carriage. He looks thin but fit, as if he just did a bunch of Crossfit and only drinks protein shakes.

His wife is at the Maison in Champagne. The house has fallen into disrepair. She's been fighting off creditors, and was thinking about selling the property just to make ends meet.
Her hands are calloused from working the vineyards, her hair is tangled, but her eyelashes have never looked better.

As Charlie enters the house, she runs to him from camera right.
She pounds her fists against his chest.

Charlie looks deeps into her eyes:
"As God is my witness, I will fix this!"

Then there's a sex scene.
It's steamy, it's hot, it's a little dirty, there is caressing.

CUT TO THE NEXT MORNING
A letter arrives.
Narrated in V.O. ideally by Michael Fassbender (Can we get his agent on the phone?)

Charles, I am the brother of your agent in New York, the one who'd refused to pay his debts. I feel terrible for what was done to you, and I wish to make amends. I am sending you a fat stack of deeds to some land in Colorado. Be well, and take care

(Fun fact: these deeds ended up being one-third of Denver. Yay, skiing!)

They are saved!
We see a slow montage of Charlie paying off his debts with the deeds, restoring the House of Charles Heidsieck, and rebuilding the winery.

Cut to a sweeping wide shot of the vineyards at dawn, smoke rising from the chimney, and Charles walking through the fields with his dog.

Make a note, dog should be cast as a hound.

THE ONES YOU KNOW

For a lot of Champagne lovers, big houses and brands are the only ones they know. It's understandable as these giants are some of the oldest houses in Champagne, and make up the majority of Champagne that is exported. For their non-vintage wines, they are all about creating a house style that is the same from year to year. As much as I don't often find myself drinking those, I really respect the tête de cuvées from these maisons, where the chef de cave (aka top dog winemaker) gets to shine in great vintages using their best grapes. It's very important to know that grower Champagne couldn't exist without the maisons paving the way, and maisons couldn't produce the amount of wine that they do without growers.

Billecart-Salmon
Cuvée Elizabeth Rose
Blend: Pinot Noir + Chardonnay
Mareuil-sur-Ay
Fresh Figs
🍕🍕🍕

Ruinart
Blanc de Blanc
Blanc de Blanc: 100% Chardonnay
Reims
Toasted baguette
🍕🍕🍕

Veuve Clicquot
Grande Dame
Blend: Pinot Noir + Chardonnay
Reims
Yellow peaches
🍕🍕🍕🍕🍕🍕

Moet
Cuvée Chalk
Blend: Pinot Noir + Chardonnay
Épernay
Blackberry sablé tart
🍕🍕🍕 1/2

Pommery
Cuvée Louis
Blend: Pinot Noir + Chardonnay
Reims
White peach cobbler
🍕🍕🍕🍕🍕🍕

Dom Pérignon
P3
Blend: Pinot Noir + Chardonnay
Hautvillers
Toasted white bread
🍕 x 240

Roederer
Brut Nature Philippe Starck
Blend: Pinot Noir + Chardonnay +
Pinot Meunier
Reims
Lemon creme fraiche
🍕🍕🍕🍕

EVENTS WHERE CHAMPAGNE (OR SPARKLING WINE) IS APPRO-PRIATE

Over the years, I have thrown a ton of parties centered around one main event: let's open gallons of Champagne. Fun fact: everyone has a good time when the bubbles are flowing.

I also have experienced extreme generosity from winemakers who have invited me into their home and cooked me some of the most memorable meals of my lifetime.

I met Jérôme Legras, winemaker and low-key amazing chef at a party in NYC many years ago. He spoke incredible English and has a very cool, confident, and welcoming way about him. He's an amazing entertainer. We met in some little bar in the West Village, my territory. He invited me to visit his house the next time I was in Champagne for dinner, his territory.

There is nothing more special than being invited to someone's home, and having them cook dinner for you. This has become a tradition of ours and over time our lives have grown and changed. He was then a bachelor and is now a married man with a baby. His wife, Charlotte, indulges in the same sense of hospitality. We have had countless conversations about life and politics and the cultural shifts in the region of Champagne. There were always other party guests, like winemakers. Jerome would always open his cellars to his own family estate, Legrass et Haas, as well as his personal cellar, because at the end of the day we are wine lovers first—and no great meal can truly exist without four to ten great bottles of wine!

If you can't party with a winemaker in Champagne, here are some parties you can throw for yourselves and your friends, based off of ones I have thrown over the years.

PARTY LIKE IT'S 1999 OR 2008 NEW YEAR'S PARTY
1999 x 2008 Vintage Champagne, Decadence, Dancing

WINE MENU
Marcel Moineaux Blanc de Blanc '08
Camille Saves Millesime '08
Jean Velut Tremolage 2008
Debolt et Vallois '08
Billecart Salmon Cuvee Nicholas 1999
Pascal Doquet BdB '99
Plus whatever else I can get my hands on.

FOOD MENU
Caviar
Cheese
Charcuterie
Lobster tails
Spreads
Etc.

Hell will freeze over at the strike of midnight ('shya right, and monkeys will fly outta my butt).And what's better than celebrating the turn of the century or 2008, when the economy crashed. We cried cash money tears and drank all the booze while bonding over simpler times.

Come indulge in the wines of 1999 and 2008, dressed as you were in these celebratory years. Plus all the lavish decadence we can find food-wise.

MUSIC: The playlist will be a mix of throwback jams (all the hits) and will blow your mind enough to leave 2016 behind!

WHEN: NYE

BALLER BUBBLES

COURSE № 1

TATTINGER COMTES DE CHAMPAGNE 2005
CAVIAR
CREME FRAICHE. POTATO CHIPS

COURSE № 3

DOM PERIGNON VINTAGE 2006
FRIED CHICKEN
SECHUAN CHILI AND HONEY MUSTARD

COURSE № 2

J.L. VERGNON BLANC DE BLANC
TOASTS
AVOCADO. CAULIFLOWER.
MUSHROOM PATE

COURSE № 4

MOËT CHALK 2002
CHURROS WITH PEACHES AND CREAM

The history of hip·hop through champagne

1980
BRANSON B. IS DUBBED THE
UNOFFICIAL SOMMELIER OF CHAMPAGNE.
SCOURING THE BACK ROOMS OF HARLEM
LIQUOR STORES FOR OLD VINTAGES

1984
"AND THEN WE TALKIN AUTOGRAPH.
AND HERE'S THE LAUGH.
CHAMPAGNE CAVIAR. AND BUBBLE BATH"
- RUN DMC. "SUCKER M.C.'S"

1985
"I WAS ALWAYS FAMOUS. BUT NEVER A STAR
A DON JUAN PERIGNON. BOURGEOIS"
- GRANDMASTER MELLE MEL. "KING OF THE STREETS"

1985
"SUN ROOF. ROLLS ROYCE. AND THE CAVIAR / FINE WINE.
CHAMPAGNE. DOM PERIGNON / SPARKLY LIKE CRAZY TO THE BREAK
OF DAWN." - KRS·ONE AND LEVI 167. "SUCCESS IS THE WORD"

1986
THE BEASTIE BOYS MENTION MOËT IN "LICENSED TO ILL"

1991
"THE WORLD'S INSANE.
WHILE YOU DRINK CHAMPAGNE"
- ICE T. "BODY COUNT"

1994
"YO. THEY CALL ME NAS. I'M NOT YOUR LEGAL TYPE OF FELLA /
MOËT·DRINKING. MARIJUANA·SMOKING STREET DWELLER."
- NAS. "REPRESENT"

1994
"BIRTHDAYS WAS THE WORST DAYS
NOW WE SIP CHAMPAGNE WHEN WE THIRST·AY"
- NOTORIOUS B.I.G.. "JUICY"

1995
"THE KING ADROCK THAT IS MY NAME
AND I KNOW THE FLY SPOT WHERE THEY GOT
THE CHAMPAGNE"
- BEASTIE BOYS. "PAUL REVERE"

1996
"AIN'T NUTTIN BUT A GANGSTA PARTY / BREAK OUT THE CHAMPAGNE
GLASSES" - TUPAC. "2 OF AMERIKAZ MOST WANTED"

1996
"KIM SURPASS ALL CREWS / BITCHES STILL DRINKIN' BOOZE / I SIP
CRISTAL AND LANDCRUISE." - LIL KIM. "DRUGS"

1999
"LET'S TAKE THE DOUGH AND STAY REAL JIGGY. UH HUH
AND SIP THE CRIS. AND GET PISSY·PISSY."
- JAY Z. "HARD KNOCK LIFE"

2000
JAY Z BECOMES UNOFFICIAL BRAND AMBASSADOR FOR ROEDERER.
CRISTAL BY RAPPING ABOUT IT IN "BIG PIMPIN"

2008
"FLASH IN MY PLAYA'S CAR (WHY YOU PLAY SO HARD?) / CUZ I'M A
DON. SIPPIN' MOËT. SMOKIN' CHRON." - SNOOP DOGG. "STOPLIGHT"

2010
"WHERE THE SUN IS ALWAYS OUT AND YOU NEVER GET OLD /
AND THE CHAMPAGNE'S ALWAYS COLD" - JAY Z. "YOUNG FOREVER"

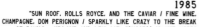

FOOD: CHEF NINI NGUYEN | BUBBLES: ARIEL ARCE
#BALLERBUBBLES
TheChampagneParlor.com

BALLER BUBBLES
The History of Hip Hop through Champagne

In the 1980s, the Hip-Hop Revolution was popping and one man, Branson B., dubbed by Forbes "The Unofficial Sommelier of Hip-Hop," was discovering the best bubbly he could get his hands on in the back cellars of Harlem's liquor stores and introducing them to the likes of Notorious B.I.G. and Sean Combs (aka Puff Daddy, aka P. Diddy, aka Diddy). The relationship between Champagne and the hip-hop community exploded, and over the last forty years, big brand wines have worked their way into hip hop culture as emblems for success.

SO LET'S BALL OUT! Baller Bubbles will explore the history of Champagnes and hip-hop coupled with grower Champagnes made in similar style or vintage. So from the lyrical stylings of Jay-Z: "Let's take the dough and stay real jiggy, uh-huh / And sip the Cris and get pissy-pissy, uh huh."

PLAYLIST:
Hip-hop from Notorious B.I.G., Tupac, Beastie Boys, Jay-Z, Red Man, Sean Puffy Combs etc.

1ST: Vilmart et Cie Grand Cellier, Rilly-la-Montagne
Winemaker: Laurent Champs

HIP-HOP ARTIST:
Branson B.

2ND: Louis Roederer "Cristal" Brut 2005, Reims
Winemaker: Jean-Baptiste Lecaillon

Artist: Jay-Z

3RD: Pierre Gimonnet Oenophile 2008 Extra Brut, Cuis
Winemaker: Pierre Gimonnet

Artist: Notorious B.I.G.

4TH: Dom Perignon Blanc 2004 Vintage, Hautvillers
Winemaker: Richard Geoffroy

Artist: Sean "Puffy" Combs

CHAMPAGNE OMAKASE
X
TOKYO RECORD BAR

You're going to need a record player.
Find a friend who likes to man the
needle.
Tell friends they can bring records if
you have special requests.

Jiro didn't dream of Champagne,
but we do.
We also like to dance, or nod our
heads uncontrollably to the musical
genres of Blues, Hip-Hop, Soul,
Jazz, Funk, Afro Beat, etc.
So in the theme of Japan's famous Record Bars, there will be an eclectic mix
of music paired with curated Champagnes customized to your palate.

If there is enough interest, Ikebana
classes can be made available.

BYO Nikka.
Tokyo Drift Drag Race to commence
at 2am.

MENU
Snax
Togarashi Popcorn
Spicy Pickles
Fluke Crudo with Yuzu
Oysters with Shiso
Crab Pea Soup
Matcha Crème Brûlée

WINES
Dhondt Grellet Terres Fines Blanc de
Blanc

Hure Frere Insousance Rose

Benoit Dehu Initiation Blanc
de Noir

DIRTY DANCING CHAMPAGNE
The history of Champagne through the '60s

How many times have you attempted that iconic lift after
too many glasses of bubbly?
Have you ever carried a watermelon?
It's 1963 and Frances "Baby" Houseman is just one listless
summer away from joining the Peace Corps. Picture the
Catskills, and Patrick Swayze's pants are so tight it hurts.
So grab your girlfriends and join The Champagne Parlor
as we blast the best soundtrack of all time paired with
country club classics and a discussion on the Champagne
industry and what was happening in 1960s American
Wine Culture.
There may be a conga line and a secret dance party
where everyone is filthy hot and sweaty, but one thing is
for sure, nobody is putting Baby in the corner.

PLAYLIST:
Dirty Dancing soundtrack and the best tracks from the
'60s

ATTIRE:
Choose what Baby you are: Pre-Kellerman's or end-of-
summer sexy . . . or maybe you're a Penny. Either way.

MENU

1ST COURSE:
Champagne Suenen Blanc de Blanc, Cramant
Shrimp Cocktail

2ND COURSE:
Camille Saves Rose, Bouzy
Caesar Salad

3RD:
Veuve Clicquot Ponsardin 2004, Reims
Fondue

4TH:
Vazart Coquart & Fils Foie Gras, Chouilly

LA CHAMPAGNERIA

Dia de Muertos

Margaritas Champagne
Royaled

Tacos

Flower Crowns

Face Painting

RARE IS RARE

Why: Because . . .
How often do you get to drink Vintage Champagne
on a Wednesday? So sit classy and sassy, because
I have procured some crazy cool and rare sparklers
to help us delve deep into conversation on vintage,
style, and maturation.

Unique Varietal, Check!

Vintage, Check!

Limited Quantity, Triple Check!

This event is all about the wine, but I would be
damned not to pair these special sparklers with
decadent treats like Cured Fishes, Cheese, Charcuterie, and Home-Baked Desserts. Expect a
special appearance from an Oenotheque, Special
Club, and Magnum.

MENU

1ST: Pierre Gerbais "L'Original" 100% Pinot Blanc,
Celles-sur-Ource
Winemaker: Aurelien Gerbais
Salmon Rillettes Smorgasbord

2ND: Bruno Paillard Assemblage 2004, Reims
Winemaker: Bruno Paillard, Laurent Guyot et Alice
Paillard
Langress with Apricots & Champagne

3RD: Vazart Coquart 2008 Special Club, Chouilly
Winemaker: Jean-Pierre Vazart
Charcuterie, Pickles, Mustard

4TH: Lanson Gold Cuvée 1999, Magnum, Reims
Winemaker: Herve Dantan
Citrus Tart & Cookies

THE CHAMPAGNE CANON: A MOVIE NIGHT

In the theatrical canon of Champagne there are plenty of cult classics that position fizz with favor.
It would be predictable to include James Bond, but don't worry, there is an entire evening dedicated to that cheeky bastard coming up soon.
Of course there is Hitchcock's *Champagne*, my girl Natalie Portman in *The Professional*, and let us not forget not one but two smoke shows: Leo and Rob Redford in *The Great Gatsby*.

I think it would be shameful to pass over films worthy of the Criterion Collection of **CHAMPAGNE**:
Wayne's World
Breakfast at Tiffany's
Rushmore
and
Four Rooms

So join me for a night of classic flicks, epic soundtracks, pretty decent Champagne, and an evening of breakfast for dinner because . . .
"I saved Latin. What did you ever do?"

Playlist: '50s, '60s, '70s, and '80s, plus the soundtracks of Wes Anderson and Quentin Tarantino.

Attire: Classy

MENU

1ST COURSE: *Wayne's World*
Etienne Calsac Revenants
Pigs in a Blanket

2ND: *Rushmore*
Champagne Cocktails
A Gentleman's Breakfast

3RD: *Breakfast at Tiffany's*
R. Pouillon Rose Brut, Maureil-sur-AY
Oeufs en Cocotte

4TH: *Four Rooms*
Krug Grand Cuvée, Reims
Ice Cream Sundaes

GET READY FOR SOME SPARKLING

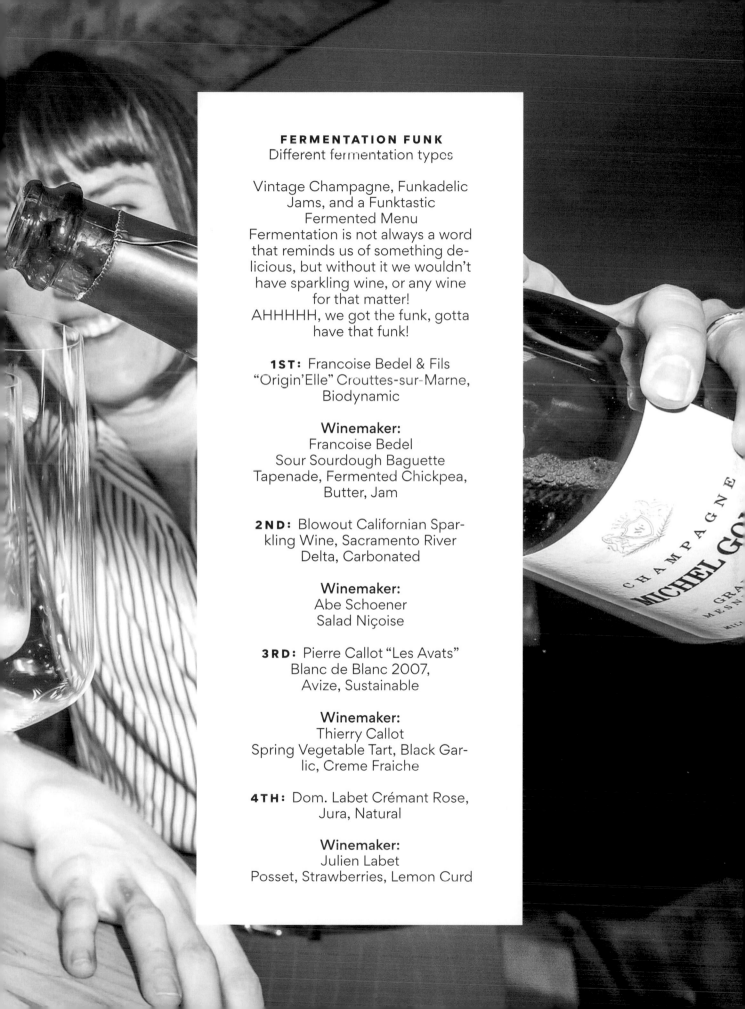

FERMENTATION FUNK
Different fermentation types

Vintage Champagne, Funkadelic Jams, and a Funktastic Fermented Menu
Fermentation is not always a word that reminds us of something delicious, but without it we wouldn't have sparkling wine, or any wine for that matter!
AHHHHH, we got the funk, gotta have that funk!

1ST: Francoise Bedel & Fils "Origin'Elle" Crouttes-sur-Marne, Biodynamic

Winemaker:
Francoise Bedel
Sour Sourdough Baguette
Tapenade, Fermented Chickpea, Butter, Jam

2ND: Blowout Californian Sparkling Wine, Sacramento River Delta, Carbonated

Winemaker:
Abe Schoener
Salad Niçoise

3RD: Pierre Callot "Les Avats" Blanc de Blanc 2007, Avize, Sustainable

Winemaker:
Thierry Callot
Spring Vegetable Tart, Black Garlic, Creme Fraiche

4TH: Dom. Labet Crémant Rose, Jura, Natural

Winemaker:
Julien Labet
Posset, Strawberries, Lemon Curd

CHAM-PAGNE

←————

SPAR-KLING

→

HEY GUYS, THANKS FOR JOINING ME OVER HERE IN THE WIDE WORLD OF EFFERVESCENCE.

I am currently sitting in the newly opened TWA hotel at New York City's JFK airport. I came out here on a whim, as I have done most things, and it's a fitting setting for what I am about to do: pick a place in the world at random to discover what sparkling wine it has to offer. If you're thinking, "But Ariel, I thought you only drank Champagne!" you would have thought right. But after ten years and thousands of glasses and a few too many bottles, it's time to step outside of Champagne and explore the rest of the world.

If you are starting here, you might be like, *wait… Champagne… I've heard of this place… what's the deal?* To you I say, close this book, and start from the beginning.

If you've already made it through Champagne and my silly stories, crazy experiences, and technical metaphors and are still game for more—let's travel to some new territories and discover some new places. So, where you flying today, Ariel?

Give me a villa in Italy or the white huts of Santorini and I might as well die and go to heaven. Yet I'm kinda embarrassed to say it, but I was very late to the party when it comes to any sparkling wine outside of Champagne. For many years I just wasn't interested, and now I am constantly playing catch up as the rest of the world grows in sparkling production.

Many bubbles throughout Europe and the rest of the world share similarities, especially when vineyards are close to the border of another country. For example, the south of France and Spain overlap in varietals, as does Spain with Portugal where those countries touch. Germany and France have some varietal blending because throughout history, the boundaries between them have gone back and forth many times (So much so that some people don't know that Alsace is actually in France!)

But traveling also allows us as wine lovers to see differences in how sparkling is made. For example, in the Canary Islands, they make sparkling from vines that grow out of deep pits in volcanic soil. (The beaches are incredible too, so win win!) Then there are places on opposite sides of the world, with very different winemaking traditions (some with very little "tradition" at all) that grow the same varietals because they have similar climates. The Willamette Valley of Oregon is said to grow pinot noir for their sparkling that's similar to Burgundy's. How is that possible? Because they have the same latitude, and share a cool, northern climate and a terroir with a dense mineral deposit.

Basically what I am getting at is that if you want to understand sparkling you gotta try it all, see it all, and then decide for yourself what you like. Like I've said before, there is a lot of great and a lot of bad, but you only got one mouth, so start using it.

GETTING ACQUAINTED WITH SPARKLING

+ SOME FUN FACTS TO KNOW

SPARKLING PRODUCTION METHODS FROM AROUND THE WORLD

I'll break down some classic methods for sparkling wines.

MÉTHODE TRADITIONNELLE

Everywhere in the world that makes sparkling wine employs *méthode champenoise*. (For how to make Champagne, see page 27.) However, when these wines are made outside of Champagne, the proper term for the process is *méthode traditionnelle*. It's too easy to compare a *méthode traditionnelle* sparkling wine—even an exceptional one—to one made in Champagne and see what it lacks. This often turns into a conversation about price comparability and quality, but you can't lose sight of the fact that other regions make excellent wines in the traditional method.

Just as in Champagne, a *méthode traditionnelle* sparkling wine goes through two fermentation processes and is aged for a period of time on its lees. But each country that produces a sparkling wine has its own rules and regulations about manual harvesting, pressing, age requirements, and other production techniques.

These rules can be less strict than Champagne's, or sometimes there are no rules at all, which can mean—at worst—inconsistent quality and—at best—wildly special wines. It's true that Champagne can only come from Champagne, but there are so many other cool categories that have little or nothing to do with *méthode traditionnelle* and turn me on:

* Ancestral method, or *pétillant-naturel*
* Prosecco
* Lambrusco
* Espumante
* Pezsgő

I can appreciate when a producer creates exceptional sparkling using *méthode traditionnelle*, but I often find myself drifting toward sparklings that are made in a regions with their own unique techniques.

CHARMAT OR TANK METHOD

During the Charmat, or tank, method, the wine is not placed into separate bottles and fermented individually as it is in the traditional method. Instead, the *liqueur de tirage* is added to a pressurized tank of still wine, which undergoes secondary fermentation. When the yeasts die, or when the winemaker decides to stop fermentation by cooling the tank, the wine is filtered and bottled without extended contact with the lees. Instead of emphasizing a wine's richness and complexity, the tank method enhances clean fruit and aromatics, making wines that are youthful and easy to drink. The most famous Charmat-method sparklers come from Prosecco.

TRANSFER METHOD

The transfer method is a hybrid of the traditional and tank methods, borrowing elements from each. These sparkling wines begin just like traditional-method sparklers, with secondary fermentation taking place inside of each bottle. Then the bottles are emptied into a pressurized tank, the wine's sediment is filtered off, and the wine is packaged in new bottles. These sparkling wines get the benefits of lees-aging without the expense or time of riddling and disgorgement. If a bubbly that would normally be made in the traditional method needs to be produced in extremely large quantities, the transfer method is used in order to ensure consistency.

CONTINUOUS METHOD

Not commonly used outside of bulk German Sekt production, the continuous method, developed in Russia, is similar to the tank method. The *liqueur de tirage* is continuously added to base wine that is pumped through a series of pressurized tanks, some of which contain oak shavings or chips. Lees accumulate on these wood shavings, enhancing toasty, yeasty flavors while also helping clarify the finished sparkling wine.

ANCESTRAL METHOD
or *Pétillant-Naturel* (or Pét-Nat, to Be Cute)

The oldest sparkling winemaking method of all, the fittingly named ancestral method, or *pétillant-naturel*, has recently regained its popularity among the wine trade. The ancestral method does not have a secondary fermentation; instead, before the first fermentation is complete, the wine is transferred from tank to bottle, where it finishes fermenting under the cork or cap. Some winemakers disgorge and rebottle ancestral-method sparkling wines after fermentation is complete, but many today elect not to, resulting in a cloudy, earthy, textured wine.

CARBONATION

This method involves carbonating a still wine using an injection of carbon dioxide, just as you do when making soda. Lest you think that it might be a clever idea to pop a bottle of still wine into a SodaStream, know that carbonation is generally considered to be an inferior method of making sparkling wine, as the bubbles dissipate quickly.

Au Naturale in the World of Sparkling

Pét-Nats, or natural sparkling wines, are booming in today's market. While this term is French AF, other regions have appropriated it, so now you can ask for a Pét-Nat and get a wine from anywhere in the world. Pét-Nats are not origin controlled but they are about hands-off winemaking—putting quality unadulterated grape juice into a bottle and letting it do its thing. These wines are often less expensive than the typical sparkler, although some have highway-robbery price tags.

There is something very alluring about a natural wine—it is what it is. Its value lies in its lack of manipulation and its purity. Pét-Nats are more about thoughtful approaches to farming and treating the grape than the winemaking after the grape is harvested from vine.

There are massively strict laws in Spain, Italy, and France for still wine production, but sparkling wine production can slide under the radar, which makes for some incredibly interesting sparklings. Generally speaking though, where there *are* rules, they fall under these statutes:

AOC
Appellation d'origine contrôlée (Appellation of Controlled Origin)
The French government created AOCs in 1935 to protect France's economic interests. Each wine-growing region of France has its own strict (or not-so-strict) regulations that must be followed in order for winemakers to be able to use the AOC on a wine label. Wines must be made from certain grapes and produced according to the regulations of each AOC.

DOC
Denominazione d'origine controllata (Designation of Controlled Origin)
The Italiano version of AOC, it's basically the same deal, just said with an Italian accent.

DOP
Or DO Denominación de Origen Protegida (Protection of Denomination of Origin)
Same here, for Spain.

AVA
American Viticulture Area (in other words, an area where one can cultivate vines)
AVA has nothing to do with regulations or production techniques and everything to do with grapes. If a winery wants AVA status for a wine label, 85 percent of the grapes in the bottle must come from the designated AVA. (Fun fact: Every state in the United States technically produces wine. Some year, on election night, I want to procure a wine from every state and taste them as the voting polls come in.)

There are other systems around the world that are explained in each region's section and also a few regions that don't have established regulations for production (or even heavily enforced rules). While regulations reinforce quality standards, they also tend to dampen creativity. Some countries are fighting these restrictions and their winemaking is undergoing some radical changes as a result.

Let's delve deeper into each region. I am so excited to take you on this journey!

CALIFORNIA CHAMPAGNE?

On the other side of this book, I emphasized Champagne as being a product. Champagne the place is also a brand, and since 1941, its economic interests have been protected by the CIVC (Le Comité Interprofessionnel du vin de Champagne, or the Comité Champagne). Champagne is protected as an Appellation d'Origine Contrôllé (Appellation of Controlled Origin, or AOC), per the 1919 Treaty of Versailles, after World War I. The writers entered a clause into the treaty to safeguard France's regional appellation, intending to protect Champagne from the Germans. The United States agreed to these terms, but never actually signed the damn thing, making the States' agreement null and void, which opened a sneaky, unintentional loophole for the USA to produce their own "Champagne." The French were so pissed (and so were many other countries looking to protect their AOCs as well as open up new trade negotiations for distribution and importation) that not until 1983 did negotiations pick back up again. It took about twenty more years for the deal to get signed, with France finally agreeing that producers in California were permitted to continue using the name "Champagne"—as long as the word "California" came after it and the wines were produced prior to 2006.

FRA

NCE

I think of French sparkling as a little bulldog lapping up a bowl of bubbles. Or a red-lipped woman in Courrèges and dark Celine sunglasses, smoking a cigarette, with black pinstripe pants and white Supergas—classique! Sparkling just screams French and it should: they drink a ton of it! The French produce 20 percent of the world's sparkling wine. Between Champagne + Crémant + Vin Mousseux + *pétillant-naturel*, they are beasts in this category!

Bénédicte et Stéphane Tissot,
Crément du Jura Rosé
Jura

CRÉMANT

Let's start with the most well-known sparkling style—CRÉMANT!

Outside of Champagne, which I call the Big C, there is the region I call the Little C—Crémant—which actually makes more wine than the Big C. It's like when a very large man gets the nickname "Shorty."

Crémant is a style of French wine made from specific grapes from nine regions, eight in France and one in Luxembourg. All Crémants are French (except Luxembourg's), but not all French sparkling wines are Crémant.

These regions are:
* Loire
* Alsace
* Burgundy
* Bordeaux
* Jura
* Savoie
* Luxembourg
* Die
* Limoux

Crémant's style of production has shorter aging periods and uses different grapes than Champagne's. There are also some similarities, such as harvesting grapes by hand and regulations that limit the amount of juice that can be extracted from each pressing. (For more about Champagne pressing, see page 27.) When producing Crémant, a winemaker may only extract one hundred liters of juice per every 150 kilograms of grapes. This selective and regulated pressing process ensures only the best juice is used.

Note that the nine regions allowed to produce Crémant also make other types of sparkling wines. In each region, you may have a producer making *pétillant-naturel* or *méthode traditionnelle.*

LOIRE

The largest sparkling region outside of Champagne, the Loire Valley is located smackdab in the middle of France. Within it two main areas produce sparkling: Anjou-Saumur and Touraine.

From the midpoint of the Valley (no, there are no valley girls), is Anjou-Saumur, where almost half of the region's sparkling—Crémant de la Loire—is produced. Halfway to Anjou-Saumur, you will hit Touraine, which is known for Vouvray and making it sparkle! These wines are made *méthode traditionnelle* and range from incredibly effervescent all the way down to a soft fizz.

GRAPES: Chenin Blanc, Cabernet Franc, Pinot Noir, Chardonnay, Cabernet Sauvignon, Arbois, Pineau d'Aunis, Grolleau, Grolleau Gris

 RECOMMENDATIONS

Château de Bois-Brinçon 2015 Brut Nature
Crémant de Loire (Anjou)
Chenin Blanc, Cabernet Franc

St. Landor Crémant de Loire (Saumur)
Chenin Blanc, Chardonnay, Cabernet Franc

Domaine de la Taille aux Loups
Chenin Blanc
Montlouis-sur-Loire

Domaine François Chidaine
Méthode Traditionnelle Brut Nature
Chenin Blanc
Biodynamic
Montlouis-sur-Loire

Jo Landron "Atmospheres"
Mousseaux
Folle Blanche, Pinot Noir
Muscat Sevre et Maine

Francois Pinon
Méthode traditionnelle, Non-Dose
Chenin Blanc
Vouvray

Catherine et Pierre Breton "La Dilettante"
Méthode traditionnelle
Chenin Blanc
Aged eleven months on lees; no sulfites added
Vouvray

Burgundy, Burgundy, Burgundy . . . Ron Burgundy? Nope, but totally just as classy. France is such a fun region to discuss because people have written entire novels, odes, and love letters to each individual region. Burgundy is the golden child, the birthplace of terroir wines, and possibly the most complex and complicated wine region in the world. It has two main grapes that have had the wine world reeling for hundreds of years—it also happens to share those two main grapes in common with Champagne: Pinot Noir and Chardonnay. While Burgundian sparkling wine can include blends of other grapes, and some Burgundian sparkling producers get as into the nitty-gritty as the top-tier still producers, Burgundy will always be known first and foremost for their non-effervescent wines. This is not a region where you are going to find a bunch of funky, natural, alternative wines. This is the classics baby, and it's rare in this region that a sparkling is not made Crémant de Bourgone.

GRAPES: Chardonnay, Pinot Noir, Alligote, Gamay. Sometimes Pinot Blanc, Sacy, Pinot Gris, Melon de Bourgogne
Rosé: Pinot Noir. Sometimes Gamay

RECOMMENDATIONS
Domaine Bruno Dangin Blanc de Noir NV
Pinot Noir
Organic
Biodynamic
Sustainable
Molesme
Crémant de Bourgogne

J.L Moissenet-Bonnard Pommard
Pinot Noir
Cote de Nuit
Sustainable
Crémant de Bourgogne

Clotilde Davenne Brut
Pinot Noir, Chardonnay
Chablis
Crémant de Bourgogne

Franck Besson Sparkling Rosé Granit
Gamay
Organic
Beaujolais
Méthode traditionnelle

The home of sweet Sauternes and Thomas Jefferson's wine escapades, Bordeaux is the foundation for any Old World wine drinker. But we aren't here to discuss first- and second-growth houses; rather, the merits of bubbles with high tannic varietals is our topic of choice. In Bordeaux, sparklings are not superabundant. The grapes fetch a better price when used in still wine, but there is a growing demand for sparkling Rosés, which fare well in this region, with such fun red varietals as Merlot, Cabernet Franc, and Cabernet Sauvignon. Mandated in Bordeaux is the grapes must be harvested by hand and there must be a minimum of twelve months aging on the lees. These wines are perfect for big party occasions, because they can be inexpensive. "Cheap and cheerful," my mom would always say.

GRAPES: Merlot, Cabernet Franc, Cabernet Sauvignon, Carménère, Malbec, Petit Verdot, Sauvignon Blanc, Semillon, Muscadelle

RECOMMENDATIONS
Jaillance Crémant de Bordeaux Brut Rosé
Merlot
Crémant de Bordeaux

ALSACE

Such an amazing wine region—and totally confusing, mainly because since forever people didn't know what it was: French? German? Swiss? The region has flipped back and forth so many times it's hard to keep track, and the culture of the people, food, and grapes reflect that fun hodgepodge. One thing Alsace is? Stunning!

I'll give you a snapshot of Alsace. The Vosges mountains protect the region from rain, keeping it dry and full of sunshine. There are tons of different soils—limestone, granite, clay, schist, gravel, chalk, loess, and the local pink sandstone—all of which impact the freshness and finesse of the wine. I think of Alsatian sparklings as crystals in a glass—they have deep minerality and power. The grapes used in their sparklings reflect their blend of French and German heritage.

GRAPES: Pinot Blanc, Auxerrois Blanc, Pinot Gris, Riesling, Chardonnay, Pinot Noir
Rosé: The AOC mandates that Rosé can only be made from Pinot Noir

Alsace has Grand Crus and classifies them in a similar way to how Burgundy classifies their Crus, labeling a village rather than a site as Premier or Grand Cru. It's rare that sparkling wines will be classified as such, as they are often blended with multiple grapes from multiple sites.

RECOMMENDATIONS
Albert Mann, Crémant d'Alsace
Auxerrois Blanc, Pinot Blanc, Pinot Noir
Biodynamic practicing

**Domaine Valentin Zusslin,
Crémant d'Alsace Brut Zéro**
Auxerrois Blanc, Chardonnay, Riesling
Organic, Biodynamic practicing, no sulfites added

Domaine François Schmitt, Crémant d'Alsace
Blanc de Noirs Brut, Zero Dosage
Pinot Noir
Organic practicing

FUCKING TART FLAMBÉ
So I have a real problem with France: the pizza is terrible. On what planet do I want raclette and Brie and Emmental on a pizza? French pizza sauce is always too sweet, and the crust is too thick and doughy, like a bagel. It's a hardship for me to go to France and not eat pizza for an extended period of time, but I have learned it's not worth buying a pizza there, even when I'm craving it.

But then I went to Colmar, Alsace, and had honest-to-goodness Tarte Flambé.

So, Tarte Flambé is not pizza, never will be pizza, isn't trying to be pizza. But maybe it's better—hot take! A perfect Tarte Flambé is thinner than a cracker but doesn't break under the weight of fromage blanc or crème fraîche, onions, and lardons.

Sure, there are no tomatoes to really satisfy the acid I'm desperate for, but the onions give a sweet acidic kick and the smoky bacon can stand its own against pepperoni cups. I would travel a solid hour out of my way for Tarte Flambé, and that's saying a lot for a girl who doesn't drive.

DIE

Sparkling wine from the Rhône Valley . . . I'm overRhôned! When sparkling wine is made from Die, it's called Clairette de Die AOC. This wine actually has a very strict mandate: a minimum of 75 percent of the blend must be made from Muscat Blanc and a maximum of 25 percent Clairette. These wines employ *méthode traditionnelle*, but their production finishes at a lower alcoholic ABV than those of Champagne and most of the rest of the world—between 7 and 8 percent versus 12 percent. These wines are intended to be drunk young, and they often taste like soft, fresh stone fruits.

 RECOMMENDATIONS
David Bautin
Muscat, Clairette
Clairette de Die
Sustainable

 JURA

When people are looking for alternative wines—something unique, a little funky cool—they often find themselves in the Jura. On the eastern side of France, Jura borders Switzerland and has a very long and cool growing season. A more remote culture, in Jura, things get done a bit differently than everywhere else in France. The still wines can be more oxidized, as they spend quite a long time in the barrel going through fermentation in the cold weather, but many of the sparkling wines are fresh and clean. The producers who make sparkling in the Jura are quite prolific still winemakers as well, and their sparklings show a hint of character, a wild and unwielding quality that is emphasized by effervescence.

GRAPES: Chardonnay, Pinot Noir, Poulsard, Savagnin, Pinot Gris, Trousseau

 RECOMMENDATIONS
Domaine Andre et Mireille Tissot
Indigène 2010
Chardonnay, Pinot Noir, Poulsard, Trousseau
Crémant du Jura

Didier Grappe Clash
Chardonnay, Savagnin
Disgorged
Pétillant-naturel

Jean François Ganevat "La Combe" Rotalier
Chardonnay
Méthode traditionnelle

BUGEY

In between Jura and the Savoie are Bugey and a little region called Bugey Cerdon, which only makes sparkling (and sometimes semi-sweet) Rosé from Gamay and Poulsard grapes. I like to think of Bugey Cerdon as Elle Woods in *Legally Blonde*: A pink, fun package that is sophisticated, smart, and knows how to throw a killer social. These wines, made via the ancestral method, clock in at only 8 percent alcohol—so hello, summer porch pounders! These wines retain a lot of their sweetness from the fruit, so no dosage is needed.

In Bugey you can also find *méthode traditionnelle* wines from Altesse and Mondeuse grapes. These wines have a powerful acidity backed up by a nutty character.

 RECOMMENDATIONS
Renardat-Fâche, Cerdon Bugey Rosé (NV)
Gamay and Poulsard
Organic

Yves Dupont Vieillissement Prolongé Brut
Montagnieu
Organic
Biodynamic
Méthode traditionnelle

SAVOIE

Savoie is one of the most recent regions to be included in the Crémant AOC. Not far from the border of Italy and nestled beautifully in between snowcapped mountains, this region is known for its bright, fresh, acidic whites. (Sound good for sparkling? I think yes!!) A minimum of 40 percent Jacquere must be present in the blend. If Altesse is included, the total percentage betweeen the two must be a minimum of 60 percent. The remaining 40 percent may include Aligote, Chardonnay, and Chasselas. There may only be 20 percent of black grapes.

GRAPES: Jacquere, Altesse, Aligote, Chasselas, Chardonnay, Gamay, Pinot Noir

 RECOMMENDATIONS
**André & Michel Quenard,
Vin de Savoie Brut** (NV)
Jacquere
Méthode traditionnelle

Domaine Giachino, Giac' Bulles Pétillant Naturel (NV)
Jacquere
Pétillant-naturel

While Luxembourg is not in France, it nevertheless gets a solid pass to use the word "Crémant." This region utilizes grapes from the Moselle River, which runs through France and Germany. Why does this region, which is not in France, get Crémant status? Well, ready for a little politics? In the late 1800s, a big Champagne brand—I won't mention any names—started to produce sparkling wine in Luxembourg, which was part of a trade collective with Germany, to avoid paying taxes on French exports to Germany. A cooperative formed after World War I tied together the sparkling production of France and Germany, and when the AOC was formed for Crémant, the cooperative, which represented the majority of sparkling wine for the region, was able to throw some weight around to get itself authorized to use the title. This benefited both France and Germany and, ya know, sometimes that's how a deal gets done.

Varietals include Pinot Blanc, Rivaner, Riesling, Elbling, Chardonnay, and Auxerrois.
Rosé: Pinot Noir

RECOMMENDATIONS
Domaine Alice Hartmann Brut
Chardonnay, Pinot Noir, Riesling
Organic
Crémant du Luxembourg

Crémant de Limoux or Blanquette de Limoux (blanquette means "small white"), made *méthode traditionnelle*, is from Languedoc but must include an indigenous varietal to the Mauzac area, also referred to as Blanquette. This generally is a small percentage and will be combined with Chardonnay and Chenin Blanc and Pinot Noir.

RECOMMENDATIONS
Domaine Les Hautes Terres
Cuvée Joséphine
Chardonnay, Mauzac
Organic
Biodynamic
Gluten-free
Sustainable
Crémant de Limoux

There are sparkling wines from Languedoc that, while not made *méthode traditionnelle*, are nonetheless beautiful expressions of a valley that is cold by night and warm by day. One family who has been committed to bringing organics to Languedoc is Mas de Daumas Gassac. This family makes long-aging whites and fruit-forward reds and produces a semi sparkler from mostly Cabernet Sauvignon. These wines taste like watermelon juice on a hot day.

RECOMMENDATIONS
Mas de Daumas Gassac
Cabernet Sauvignon, Mourvèdre, Pinot Noir, Sauvignon Blanc, Petit Manseng, and Muscat
Vin de Table
Organic

And a sparkler that doesn't fit into one of the Major 9

Sulauze Super Modeste Pet-Nat
Rolle (Vermentino)
Provence
Biodynamic
Pétillant-naturel

Clockwise from top left:

Franck Besson, Rosé Granit
Burgundy

Mas de Daumas Gassac, Rosé Frizant
Languedoc-Roussillon

Moissenet-Bonnard, Crémant de Bourgogne
Burgundy

Domaine Bornard, Tant-Mleux Petlllant Naturel
Jura

TALY

Italy is overwhelming. It's got endless specialty sparkling, a lot of which has been mistakenly and, sadly, grouped up under one word: Prosecco. But not everything that sparkles in Italy is Prosecco. There are a million varietals, many winemaking regions, tons of different types of wines, that honestly even I didn't know where to begin. But once I went down this beautiful rabbit hole, there was no going back.

The most commonly known regions for sparkling are:
* Veneto
* Lombardy
* Emilia-Romagna

And these regions also make sparkling:
* Piemonte
* Trentino-Alto Adige
* Umbria
* Marche
* Abruzzo
* Puglia
* Sicily
* Sardinia
* Tuscany
* Friuli-Venezia Giulia

There are two principal methods to making Italian sparkling. (And by now they'll sound familiar!)

1. *Metodo Classico,* aka *méthode traditionnelle*, has two fermentations, with the second fermentation (which makes the bubbles) occurring in the bottle.

2. *Metodo Italiano*, aka the Charmat or tank method, has two fermentations, both of which occur in a stainless-steel tank.

PLUS!
It's important to note two abbreviations:

DOC: Denominazione di Origine Controllata
&
DOCG: Denominazione di Origine Controllata e Garantita

DOC is a set of strict regulations introduced in 1963 after the Treaty of Rome to protect Italy's economic interests. Among regulating other Italian products, these set quality controls for production of wine: which grapes can be used and their yields, what vessels were allowed, minimum and maximum ageing, and how high the alcohol content could be.

But Italian winemakers (as well as producers of cheese, oil, and charcuterie) began to feel that the DOC was granted too liberally—they wanted a tougher standard for the finest products. In 1980, DOCG was developed to specify the top wines throughout Italy.

When we talk about sparkling, only regions in northern Italy hold DOCG status.
* Lombardia
* Franciacorta
* Oltrepo Pavese *Metodo Classico*
* Moscato di Scanzo
* Piedmont
* Barbera d'Asti
* Veneto
* Prosecco

The two most familiar sparkling wine regions are:
Franciacorta, in the province of Brescia in Lombardy, where the wines are generally made *metodo classico.*
Valdobiadenne in Veneto, where we get Prosecco made *metodo Italiano.*

The other regions produce a mixture of
Méthode traditionnelle wines
Ancestral or *pétillant-naturel* wines
Moscato d'Asti
Brachetto d'Acqui
and
Lambrusco

ATMOSPHERIC PRESSURE

I always say that opening a bottle of bubbly reveals a lot about how a person behaves under pressure. Not only are you under pressure when opening the bottle, but the juice inside is under pressure too! And you don't know what the life for the bottle has been like before it got into your hands: Has it been kept at the right temperature? Has it been shaken up? How long has it been in the bottle? All of this impacts how the bottle opens. If you don't handle it properly, it could go off at any moment. Me, it's my time to shine, but I digress.

When Champagne and sparkling wine are bottled, the liquid is not effervescent. It goes into said bottle under 5 to 6 atmospheric bars of pressure, which leaves the right amount of space within the wine to hold what will become a very intense dance party. You see, when the juice is added to the bottle with yeast and sugar and sealed shut, they start moshing together, going at it full force and grinding up against each other to make sexy CO_2. As this is happening, the CO_2 doesn't have anywhere to go. It's stuck in the bottle, pushing against the inside of the glass. The pressure that was applied to the contents of the bottle made room for this growing monster, but it's still powerful and explosive. (This sounds random, but it's all been calculated carefully: The amount of sugar and yeast added to the bottle in tandem with a specific atmospheric pressure results in different degrees of effervescence. For example, less pressure yields a semi-sparkler, or a frizzante.)

Imagine the dissolved CO_2 like gas in your tummy. The more CO_2 there is, the greater the pressure. In your stomach, it's just gas, but once that gas is released and exposed to normal atmospheric pressure, it becomes a pocket of air ... aka a fart. So think of bubbles like tiny farts waiting to happen. Once the juice is released from inside the bottle, the dissolved CO_2 mixes with normal atmospheric pressure. The CO_2 then converts itself into bubbles—and the more CO_2 in the bottle, the more bubbles there will be. Sometimes magic happens on the dance floor, and sometimes you eat too much and gotta let a little loose.

**Orsolani, Cuvée Tradizione
Metodo Classico**
Piedmont

I Clivi, RBL Brut Nature
Friuli-Venezia Giulia

LOMBARDY

FRANCIACORTA

Lombardy has been dubbed "The Champagne of Italy." Sure, it patterns its *metodo classico* production of sparkling after Champagne's (per the DOC) and utilizes grapes that are also grown in Champagne: Pinot Nero (Noir), Chardonnay, and Pinot Bianco (Blanc). But the comparison still seems a bit unfair. After all, is a region outside of Champagne that produces wine *méthode champenoise* just a copycat? If the region produced wine *méthode champenois* but used indigenous varietals, maybe it wouldn't be compared to Champagne, but the fact that Chardonnay and Pinot Noir grow so well in cold climates, which are also very good for sparkling wine, often leads connoisseurs to dub such regions "the Champagne of X."

Lombardy is much more than a "Champagne of Italy." Its mineral-rich terroir has both a limestone base that develops a finesse in its wines and a cool climate that reaches fresh levels of acidity. The wines must be aged for eighteen months on lees—just a bit longer than Champagne's fifteen months for non-vintage wines. A vintage, by law, must remain in the bottle on lees for a minimum of thirty months.

Franciacorta has some important style classifications.
* Saten means 100 percent white grapes, such as Chardonnay or Pinot Bianco. Plus the atmospheric pressure must be at 4.5 bars (lower than Champagne's 6 bars), which causes the wine to feel softer, without such powerful bubbles.
* All Rosés must have a minimum of 15 percent Pinot Nero in the blend.
* The dosage is the same as Champagne's (For more about Champagne's dosage, see page 41).
* The original producer was Guido Berluchi, who is credited with bringing the style of *metodo classico* to Franciacorta in the 1950s. Many larger producers from this region such as Bellavista, Ferrari and Ca' del Boscom make up the majority of the spumante (Italian sparkling wine) from this area.
* The price point of these sparklings can vary but they often are the more expensive Italian sparkling wines.

RECOMMENDATIONS
Monte Rossa, Franciacorta
Prima Cuvée Brut
Chardonnay, Pinot Nero, Pinot Blanc
Aged twenty months on lees
Half aged in stainless-steel tanks and half aged in natural oak vessels

Ricci Curbastro Brut Satèn 2014
100 percent Chardonnay, all estate fruit
Aged forty months on lees
Aged in new and second-used* French oak

* Winemakers actually don't choose to use old barrels to impart a wood flavor to the wine but as a way to allow the wine to have more contact with the elements, such as in creating a more oxidative style. The wood of older oak barrels has less of an impact on the wine than newer wood barrels.

METODO CLASSICO, MADE OUTSIDE FRANCIACORTA
Bruno Giacosa Spumante Extra Brut 2015
Piedmonte
Pinot Nero

Cantina Colonnella, Le Rue Passerina Brut Rosé
Abruzzo,
Montepulciano
Sustainable

Punta Crena, Colline Savonesi Mataòssu Spumante Brut
Liguria
Mataòssu
Aged nine months on lees
Malolactic fermentation

Orsolani Caluso Spumante Cuvée Tradizione
Metodo Classico
Piedmont
Erbaluce
Aged thirty-six months on lees

VENETO

PROSECCO MADE IN VALDOBBIADENE, VENETO

We all have had Prosecco, either for brunch—hold the orange juice—or at a friend's house when they say they are "popping some Champagne." It's often on a wine list under the sparkling section for around ten to twenty dollars (gasp) a glass. Its fresh style is due to its grapes' soft, white peach and berry aromas and a production method that doesn't expose the juice to air or wood or direct lees contact for extended periods of time. These wines are intended to be made fast and drunk young.

Prosecco is a delight, if you're drinking the good stuff—there is a major difference between DOC and DOCG Prosecco.

The original DOC permitted a large portion of Veneto to produce Prosecco and label it DOC. Then, in 2009, an area prized for its terroir was named the DOCG. Valdobbiadene, high in the Italian Alps, has a cool climate plus sun exposure, a combo that allows its wines to ripen with balance and finesse.

Glera is the OG grape in Prosecco made in Conefliano Valdobbiadene. A Prosecco must be comprised of a minimum of 85 percent Glera. Other grapes that make up the 15 percent remaining (like the tiny slice of cake that every person at the party is like, "Ugh not too much, just a small slice") are Pinot Bianco, Pinot Nero, Pinot Grigio, and the indigenous varietals Perera, Verdiso, and Bianchetta Trevigiana.

Every wine store carries base-level brands of Prosecco in orange or blue packaging, just as they do with brands of Champagne. Try an exercise: buy a bottle of this stuff—it should run you ten to fourteen dollars. Pour a glass and let it sit for an hour until all the bubbles have dissipated. Taste what's left, the base of the wine.

I can tell you what I taste: high acid, bitterness, cloying sweetness.

SO IF YOU WANT TO TRY SOME GREAT PROSECCOS, HERE YOU GO.

Le Vigne di Alice, Prosecco di Valdobbiadene
Superiore Brut Doro Nature
Glera, Verdiso, Bianchetta

Bisol, Prosecco Valdobbiadene Superiore di Cartizze Non Dosage
Glera

Rezzadore Prosecco DOCG
Glera
Organic

Bortolomiol "Luis Nature" Brut DOCG
Glera, Native varietals

Casa Belfi
Furlani, Bianco Frizzante
Trento-Alto Adige
Lagarino Bianco, Nosiola, and Verderbara
Biodynamic
No sulfites added
Col Fondo

THE MARTINOTTI MISERY

Ever have an idea and then all of a sudden it exists in the world and you're like, "I totally invented that?" In 1895, Federico Martinotti developed a way to produce sparkling wine via two fermentation processes. The first fermentation happened in a wooden tank, and then the juice was strained into a pressurized tank or wooden vessel where added yeast and sugar ignited the second fermentation. The whole batch was fermented at once and the effervescent wine was then bottled with its fizz.

But at the same time Martinotti was developing his method, a French daddy, Eugene Charmat, was developing the same process but using stainless-steel tanks, which produced a more consistent product. Frenchie got the patent and today we call this the Charmat method. Still referred to as the Martinotti method in Italy, this tank method is the principal technique for producing Prosecco.

Sandro de Bruno, Durello 36
Metodo Classico V.S.Q.P.R.D
Veneto

ANCESTRALE, NATURALE, OR JUST BY ACCIDENT!

The fun thing about sparkling wine is that it's more alive than any other wine. If something goes a bit south in the winemaking process, a wine can accidentally turn into frizzante. This happens once in a while, often with wines that have little to no added sulfur igniting a secondary fermentation in the bottle. A fun example is Monastero Suore Cistercensi Coenobium 2017, which accidentally but awesomely effervesced during fermentation. The wine is made by nuns in consultation with Palo Bea, a very prolific Italian natural-esque producer. It's a beautiful mistake.

RECOMMENDATIONS
Cantina Giardino, Vino Rosato Frizzante
Campagnia
Sparkling Rosé
Aglianico, Coda di Volpe, Greco, and Fiano
Natural

I Clivi, Colli Orientali del Friuli Brut Nature RBL
Ribolla Gialla
Friuli-Venezia Giulia
Organic

Castello di Tassarolo, Spinola Gavi Frizzante 2015
Cortese
Piedmonte
Organic
Biodynamic
No sulfites added

COL FONDO

Col Fondo is the *pétillant-naturel*–esque style of Italy. Broken-record time, but just to reinforce the many shared methods around the world: Col Fondo is a one-fermentation process that happens in the bottle. Col Fondo, "with the bottom," means that the yeasts are legit on the bottom of the bottle when you get the wine. There are some exceptions to this, such as when a winemaker might choose to disgorge the yeast before rebottling and selling the wine. This might be done for aesthetic reasons or because the winemaker prefers a cleaner texture or wants the wine to stop fermenting.

Emilia-Romagna is home to the modern-day patron saint Mossimo Bottura, who has made pasta so cool that a millennial foodie might make a pilgrimage to Modena just for a chance to *Lady and the Tramp* some tagliatelle. It's the birthplace of lasagna and balsamic vinegar plus Parmigiano Reggiano. And once you're super-satiated you can drive off your caloric intake in a sweet Ferrari, Maserati, or Lamborghini, all brands that call the region home. I think of Emilia-Romagna as the capital of just-fuck-it fun, so it makes perfect sense that it would also have such a unique and specialized beverage—Lambrusco—one that is so sophisticated yet rooted in simple pleasure and deliciousness.

This wine is made somewhat traditional, somewhat ancestral, or *pétillant-naturel*. Oenologists have discovered that there are up to sixty mutations of the Lambrusco grape; the most widely cultivated is Lambrusco Salamino. The juice and skins spend up to thirty-six hours together during the first fermentation, igniting a spontaneous fermentation, and the second fermentation happens in the bottle. It isn't disgorged. Depending on how long the juice and skins spend together, the wines can range from soft light pink to dark as squid ink. They can also range from incredibly dry to very sweet.

LIGHT
Moretto Grasparossa de Castelvetro Lambrusco
Rosato

MEDIUM
Denny Bini (Podere Cipolla), Lambrusco dell'Emilia
Lambrusco Marani, Lambrusco Salamino, Lambrusco Maestri, Lambrusco Grasparossa, and Ancellotta
Organic

FULL
Hodge Podge Sparkling
Mirco Mariotti, Sét e Mèz Fortana Dell'Emilia
Rosé
Fortana

JUST BELOW, IN THE MARCHE . . .
Paris Rocchi, San Ginesio Vernaccia Nera Secco
Spumante
Vernaccia Nera
Sparkling Red
Organic

PIEDMONT

FOR A LITTLE SWEETNESS
Moscato d'Asti had a moment in the limelight when hip-hop culture was showcasing the delicious, low-alcohol semi-sweet wines of Piedmont. But let's go a bit deeper. Moscato d'Asti is a sweeter-style wine made from the Moscato grape—and just because something has sweetness does not mean that it's unsophisticated! Two areas known for their sweet wine actually hold a DOCG for Asti Spumante and Brachetto d'Acqui, the latter made from a Piedmont red grape, which can also be used in sparkling Rosé. In order to have DOCG on a label, the amount of residual sugar in a sparkling wine must be 150 grams or lower, but as these grapes naturally have 170 grams of sugar, at times these wines can't be classified this way.

Carussin, Moscato d'Asti Filari Corti
Piedmont
Moscato d'Asti
Biodynamic

G.D. Vajra, Moscato d'Asti
Piedmont
Moscato
Sustainable
Vegan
This wine is made by an established family known for Nebiolo in Piedmonte.

Braida, Brachetto d'Acqui
Piedmont
Brachetto

And Who Doesn't Love An Island Wine!
* Sardus Pater, Vermentino di Sardegna *Metodo Classico* AD49
* Sardinia
* Vermentino

One-hundred-fifty-year-old vines growing in sand with myrtle, juniper. and mastic bushes and harvested by hand.

SICILY

SOUTHERN SPARKLING: MOUNT ETNA, SICILY
There are plenty of sparkling southern wines from Italy, but the most fascinating wines come from Mount Etna, an active volcano that recently erupted in 2017. The vineyards here have major mineral deposits and volcanic soil that massively impact the wines, leaving them with a spicy quality. Despite that fact the vineyard sites are in the south, they are at a high altitude, giving them a cooler climate, which allows the grapes to retain their acidity and keeps them from getting overly ripe.

Planeta Brut
Carricante
Metodo classico

I Vigneri di Salvo Foti, Etna Vinudilice Brut Rosé
Alicante, Grecanico Dorato, and Minnella
Sparkling Rosé
Metodo classico

IF YOU'RE VEGAN, ASK ABOUT YOUR WINE
Not all wines are vegan. During the fining and filtering process, an agent traditionally made from eggs or fish scales removes lingering particles. Modern-day producers may use bentonite, a clay (and no, not an animal byproduct). Time is an incredible settler as well: the longer a wine sits, the more time the particles have to settle. The wine will naturally clarify itself.

EECE

Helloooo, Greece, land of sky-blue seas, seafood you can grab out of the ocean, olive oil, never-ending sun, economic issues, white beaches, plus a club that was once helmed by Lindsay Lohan . . . RIP Lohan Beach.

Greece has been making semi sparklers for centuries, but modern-day sparkling didn't begin in Greece until the late 1960s. This wonderful place wouldn't be next on our grand tour of sparkling wine if it wasn't full of a bunch of technical information, government-mandated rules, varietals that seem impossible to pronounce, and, you guessed it, BUBBLY!!!

**Domaine Glinavos, Ioannina
Paleokerisio**
Epirus

**Domaine Karanika, Amyntaion
Brut Nature Extra Cuvée de Ré-
serve Méthode Traditionnelle**
Macedonia, Greece

Just like everywhere else Old Worldly, Greece has its PDO (Protected Designation of Origin)—gotta protect those old things guys, gotta keep 'em safe.

| AOQS | (Designations of Origins of Superior Quality) |

These are areas where indigenous varietals are protected and the rules for production are serious—including the rule that even the winery that produces the wine has to be within the mandated protected wine zone.

P.S. Why AOQS doesn't have terms starting with A-O-Q-S is beyond me. Maybe it's the Greek alphabet, which translates quite differently in English. Girl with the hands-up emoji?!

In the north you have Zitsa in Epirus, where the grape Debia started it all, and Amynedo, where the red grape Xinomovaro dominates as either Blanc de Noirs or can be blended for Rosés. In Limnos, a little island off northern coast of Greece, you see some experimentation with Assyrtiko, which is like Greece's Sauvignon Blanc. In central Greece, you have Thessaly also playing around with Assyrtiko and Xinomavaro.

In the Aegean Islands, you have Rodos, which utilizes *méthode traditionnelle* for its wines, and Santorini, where Assyrtiko and Athiri are used to create Blanc de Blancs. And in southern Greece you have Peloponnese, where Moschofilero in the vineyards of Mantinia gets nice salinic air coming off the coast that keeps the wines fresh.

Other varietals include: Vidiano, Limniora, Agiorgitko and Muscat of Alexandria

RECOMMENDATIONS
Karanika, Amyndeon Xinomavro Brut Cuvée Speciale
Macedonia, Amyndeo
Xinomavro, Assyrtiko
Méthode traditionnelle

Domaine Glinavos Paleokerisio Ioannina
Epirius
Debina, Vlahiko
Orange, Semi Sparkling

Kamara Kioutsoukis Estate, Pet-Nat
Xinomavro, Malagousia, Assyrtiko
Thessalia
Organic

Santo Santorini Brut *Méthode Traditionnelle*
Aegean Islands, Santorini
Assyrtiko

s

PAIN

Spain is one of the most exciting countries in the world for wine. If you're reading this twenty years from now, I would venture to say it'll still be pretty exciting. Everything feels so new and revolutionary even though that's due to a return of the old. The Spanish have been making sparkling wine for hundreds of years, and in fact were pioneers in inventing the gyropalette. (See page 41.) But winemaking in Spain is changing.

Clockwise from top left:

**Ramon Jane, Indoinable Brut
Nature Cava**
Penedès

**Raventós i Blanc, Textures de
Pedra Blanc de Natura**
Catalonia

**Gramona, Imperial Method
Traditional Corpinnat**
Penedès

CAVA AND CORPINNAT

Spanish sparkling has always been known strictly as Cava. This term refers to wines made *méthode traditionnelle*, employing the trinity of Spanish sparkling grapes Macabeo, Parellada, and Xarello as well as Pinot Noir and Chardonnay. Cava mainly comes from the region of Catalunya, specifically Penedès, which is thirty minutes outside Barcelona, but Cava can be made all over Spain. The word itself translates to "cave" or "cellar," which tells you what is very important to the style of Cava: ageing.

In 2019, nine important winemakers from Penedès, frustrated by the DO Cava's inadequate regulation, lackadaisical ageing requirements, and the lack of compassion many of the Cava producers had for the land, decided to leave the DO Cava and create their own union, Corpinnat. Corpinnat, or "Heart of Penedès," is designed to place on the front line of the battle for quality wines a stronger requirement for ageing in order to see deeper development and complexity and a strict dedication to biodynamic practices in the vineyards.

RECOMMENDATIONS
Gramona III Lustros Gran Reserva 2011
Xarel-lo and Macabeo
Organic
Biodynamic
Aged ninety-six months on lees
Corpinnat

Recoredo Intens Rosat 2014
86 percent Monastrell, 14 percent Garnatxa
Corpinnat

Mas Candi Indomable 2013
Xarel-lo, Sumoll
Biodynamic
Corpinnat

Eudald Massana Noya
Macabeu, Xarel-lo, and Parellada
Organic
Biodynamic
Cava

AN OLD FRIEND

I don't know if there is a box Pepe Raventós could fit in. When I met him, he must have been in his mid-forties and he had braces. Tall and handsome, he resembled a wild bird. He has five kids and an amazing wife, and he had moved them all from suburban Spain to NYC so he could personally sell his wines. He came to visit me in 2013 at Birds & Bubbles, a fried chicken restaurant we were building in the Lower East Side of NYC, for which I was the Bubbles.

When Pepe came by to let me taste his wines, my dad was in another room, building a hanging shelf unit. Halfway through Pepe's rant evangelizing Xerello, an indigenous grape used in Cava, my dad came into the room and Pepe offered him a blind taste of the next sparkling.

My father took a sniff, a sip, and mused, "Cava . . . is this vintage?"

Pepe's mouth dropped as he turned to me as if to say, "Who is this guy? How would he know?"

My dad had called the region and that it was from one specific year, when most Cavas are blends of many vintages.

Then my father was probably dressed in his classic black T-shirt and denim overalls, sporting a mane of untamed wild gray. He resembled Wario, the evil version of Mario from Super Mario games. (Or picture Albert Einstein in work clothes.) To this day I have no clue how Pops was able to blind-taste vintage Cava, but let me tell you, it scored me some major bonus points with Pepe. He invited my dad and me to visit him in Penèdes, offering to take us on a trip through the Pyrenes, where we have ancestors.

It took me five years to take him up on it, but in the summer of 2018, I went to visit the paradise of Raventós i Blanc.

Pepe the winemaker is not like everyone else. He's never followed the rules, and, from the beginning of his career, he's thought about making wine in a different way than his peers do. The estate of Raventós i Blanc has been making sparkling wine since 1872, but in 2012 Pepe decided to leave behind the Cava DO. He petitioned to start his new designation, Conca del Riu Anoia. On his estate, filled with wild hogs, forests, fields, horses, RVs, chalk quarries, herbs growing wild, he consciously created an ecosystem, with every one thing connected to another—a sense of place conveyed through his wines.

BLIND TASTING

Blind tasting is just that—a wine is presented in front of you with no information as to what it is. You taste, and you make your best guess. Sometimes this can be an ego trip, a dick-swinging contest, a way to puff up your chest and be like, "Yep, I know my shit." Most of the time when I blind taste, I swirl that glass for a while, taste the wine a few times, and then say, "Beats me." Once in a blue moon, I can pull it out of my ass. I shock myself when I realize I know what I am talking about. But then there are those blind tastings when you are in the presence of a master. Someone who just by looking, smelling, and tasting a wine can tell you where it comes from, what varietal it's made of, and even what year it was made. It's like a magic trick of the mouth. Unless it's an illusion or they peeked at the label, it's not magic at all—it's a real talent.

His mission was to create a sparkling that reflected his region, and with Penèdes producers beginning to transition from Cava to Corpinnat —a massive change in the region—I thought his revolution was coming to fruition. On my trip I said to him, "Wow, Corpinnat—finally people are coming around to your vision," and he laughed. It still wasn't enough for him. He was not Corpinnat—he was his own unique version of Spanish sparkling and he would not be classified.

As we sat in his backyard around the dinner table under the stars, there were four generations of the family at the table, tons of children running around, pups lying under our feet, brothers and sisters and mothers and grandparents, including his ninety-six-year-old grandmother. I felt I understood him then. Who wouldn't want to capture perfection in a bottle, and why would you ever let rules keep you from doing that?

RECOMMENDATIONS
Raventós i Blanc Textures de Pedra Blanc de Negra 2014
Xarel-lo Vermell, Bastard Negre, Sumoll
Biodynamic
Conca del Riu Anoia

Can Sumoi
Sumoll
Conca del Riu Anoia
Biodynamic
Pétillant-naturel
Vegan

There are other amazing sparklings going on throughout the region that are focusing on Old World traditions of ancestral method and unique varietals, some from Catalunya and others from all reaches of the country.

Clos Lentiscus
Malvasia
Penèdes
Biodynamic
No sulfites added
Pétillant-naturel
Vegan

BASQUE COUNTRY

A semi-soft, often dry sparkling hailing from the Basque and northern regions of Spain as well as, to a lesser degree, Chile, Txakoli is a drink-all-day low-alcohol selection coming in at 9.5 to 11.5 percent alcohol.

The best known of the style comes from the appellation of Getariako Txakolina, with Bizkaia and Alava producing substantially smaller quantities and different styles. It gets its bubble from a partial Charmat or tank method, in which the grapes are chilled and an indigenous yeast is added to the tank. This blanket of yeast helps retains the carbon dioxide produced during this process, making the wine bubbly.

A huge part of Basque culture, this wine is traditionally drunk young—about as young as it should be drunk! At most, the wine will spend a year in the bottle, but if you were drinking this in San Sebastián, these wines could be as young as six months old. It was created so as not to compete with red Riojas, and in this northern climate, the grapes produce a high-acid, refreshing beverage. It's the Spanish alcoholic seltzer with complexity and density—it's the Le Croix of Sparkling!!

RECOMMENDATIONS
Izar-Leku Sparkling Txakoli 2015
Ameztoi, Txakoli de Gatara Rubentis Rosé

Plus an Island Wine for good measure, because salty salinic air and bubbly does the body good.

CANARY ISLANDS

Los Bermejos Lanzarote Espumoso Brut Nature 2014
Malvasia

PORT
GAL

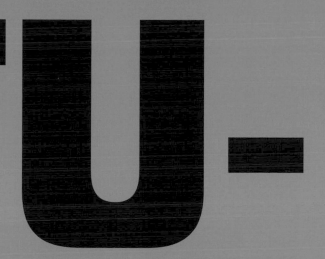

In 2012, the Portuguese board of tourism offered a European passport to anyone who invested five hundred thousand euros in property. Needless to say, tourism boomed. But even before that, Portuguese wines were becoming a hot ticket on the market. Port and Madeira were always associated with Portugal—it just wasn't known for its sparkling outside of the semi-sparkler Vinho Verde. In fact, still when I talk about Portuguese sparkling, people go, "Huh? They make that there?"

**Aphros, Vinho Verde Pet Nat
Phaunus**
Minho

**João Pato a.k.a. Duckman,
Duck Pet Nat**
Beiras

Time to take a step back and discuss the term "Espumante," which is the Portuguese sparkling moniker. Most Espumante come from Portugal, and some comes from Argentina. It's the blanket term for sparkling in those countries, and it is often injected or force carbonated with CO_2.

Portugal's largest sparkling region is Bairrada. About an hour and a half northeast of Lisbon, the region has been producing wine at a rapid rate due to the up-and-coming young gen and Bairrada DOC.

Another important sparkling region to note is in Tavora-Varosa, in northern Portugal. This region was the first in Portugal to be DOC'd for sparkling wine, in 1989. These wines commonly use the Malvasia Fina grape. A powerful grape when used in Madeira, Malvasia Fina has an incredibly dominant flavor profile. Yet, in sparkling, this grape can taste like anything from herb and mint to almond and hazelnut, from flowers and salt to peaches and nectarines. Non-indigenous varietals can grow in the northern climate of the region, so winemakers choose to make things interesting by blending the grape with traditional-for-bubbly Chardonnay and Pinot Noir to support and dilute this wild and powerful grape. This practice is an example of outside varietals being planted to replicate *méthode champenoise*, but to me, the more exciting wines use grapes indigenous to the area.

On a recent trip to Portugal, I was really blown away. Seafood tastes better there than anywhere else I have been, the weather is impeccable, the people are genuinely kind, and, no matter where you go, you can get a pretty reasonable bottle of wine. Of course, the great stuff is also available!

RECOMMENDATIONS
Aphros Phaunus
Organic, Biodynamic
Vinho Verde
Pet Nat
Loureiro

Filipa Pato 3B Rosé
Baga and Bical
Espumante
Bairrada

READY FOR SOME ACRONYMS?
When seeking out quality sparkling wines from Portugal, look for wines with these designations.

VQPRD

Vinhos de Qualidad Produzides em Regiao Determinada
VQPRD refers to wine that can be made by any method—Charmat or tank, transfer or *méthode traditionnelle*—and anywhere in Portugal.

VFQPRD

Vinho Frisante de Qualidade Produzido em Regiao Determinada
A step up is VFQPRD, which is origin controlled and can only be made in the Douro, Lisbon, Minho, Ribatejo, and Alentejo regions.

VEQPRD

Vinho Espumante de Qualidade Produzido em Regiao Determinada
This new designation is strictly for Bairrada DOP Espumante, whose grape varietals are Baga and a handful of Touriga national grapes. Grapes also permitted are Maria Fomes, Arinto, Bical, and sometimes Chardonnay. These wines must be made *méthode traditionnelle* with secondary fermentation in the bottle. The aging requirements are substantially lower than in Champagne, anywhere from four to twelve months on lees.

EAST
EURO

ERN
PE

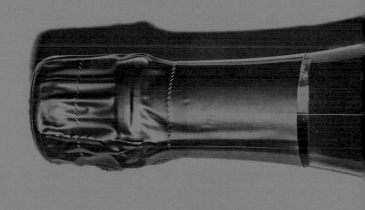

We're moving east, and hold on to your glasses—I am going to cover a lot of ground in a little space. Tons of words you probably won't be able to pronounce and styles you may have never heard of before: bubbles made *méthode traditionnelle* by Germans, Hungarian wines made Charmat-style, and natural sparklers from Austria and the Czech Republic. What I love about this area of the world is that there is everything from hyper classic wines made with indigenous varietals to off-the-wall fizz that the government doesn't want exported. Discovering sparkling here feels like being let in on a secret—and the twenty-first century is showing a lot of inspired innovation mixing with tradition. If you think fried and chicken and Champagne is a great combo, wait til you try schnitzel and Sekt.

GERMANY

Germans love sparkling wine. One of the world's largest groups of sparkling consumers, Germans know not only how to knock back bubbly from around the globe but also how to produce their own sparkling, called Sekt. Historically, Germans loved sparkling so much that in the late 1800s, many Germans, in a fit of wanderlust, traveled to Champagne to learn how to make sparkling wine. Some stayed (which is why many big-house Champagne producers don't have French-sounding names, like Krug, Bollinger, and Heidsieck) while others brought back to Germany *méthode champenois*.

Fast-forward through two terrible wars, to Germany seeking to industrialize and rebuild its economy: Sekt wine producers left *méthode champenois* and its labor-intensive in-bottle fermentation in favor of tank fermentation. There was not much investment in classifying regions and protecting the quality of German sparkling. Thankfully, priorities have changed, and once again the best of Germany's sparkling wines follow rigorous standards.

GERMANY HAS SOME VERY HARD-TO-PRONOUNCE CLASSIFIERS—JUST SOUND THEM OUT!

DEUTSCHER SEKT

Wines can only be labeled as Deutscher Sekt if they're from 100 percent German grapes. These wines may be produced via the Charmat, or tank method or *méthode traditionnelle* with a minimum of nine months on the lees.

A fair amount of German Sekt is produced from outside Germany, in Italy, France, or Spain, so if you are going for the homegrown goods, best to stick to these labels I list below. Inexpensive sparklings injected with CO2 can be easily differentiated from Sekt because these cannot be labeled as Sekt: These are called Schaumwein, which cutely translates to "foam wine." Perlwein is a semi-sparkling wine with less atmospheric pressure than that used in *méthode traditionnelle*.

SEKT B.A.
Bestimmter Anbaugebiete

This sparkling must be made from all German grapes, specifically from thirteen regions known for their quality, for example Mosel and Rheingeau.

Winzersekt

This definition of German sparkling is the fanciest of all the classifications. Wines with this label must be made with only estate fruit from a German house or winemaker. It must be aged at minimum nine months on the lees, and the label must list the grapes used and the vintage. The dominant grape for Winzersekt wines are Riesling, while alternative grapes are Pinot Noir, Chardonnay, Pinot Meunier . . . you have heard these many times before in this book! Also used are grapes that aren't as well known: Traminer & Muskateller.

You're probably thinking, "Germany . . . these guys are known for one grape above all else!"

RIESLING.

I've been waiting to get to Riesling! Many wine professionals will say I mainly drink Chardonnay, Chenin, and Riesling because they are fucking delicious, high acid, and have gorgeous texture. From incredible producers, these varietals can be ethereal. This grape is hard to mistake as anything other than riesling when you start to taste a lot of them, but its terroir can enhance its qualities. Add a great winemaker into the mix and Riesling can go down easy while still leaving you with this feeling that you drank something only special people get to drink. It's downright quaffable while being unbelievably dynamic and complex. With flavors that range from tropical to tennis balls, it can drink as thick as oil and as sweet as honey. It's a total mindfuck of a grape that still retains its identity: You always know it's Riesling but you can't always pinpoint why. It just is.

Germany's wine region, the northernmost wine climate in the world, is cold, mineral rich, and perfect for a nuanced, delicate, fruitful grape like Riesling. And it's extra amazing for sparkling Riesling.

So if we are talking about German sparkling, some of the most incredible examples are Riesling Sekt.

There are only six so-called noble grapes: Pinot Noir, Chardonnay, Sauvignon Blanc, Cabernet Sauvignon, Merlot, and—you guessed it—Riesling. These grapes are essentially the grapes that started everyone's wine obsession. Aside from Riesling, they all originated in France, but as Riesling does exceptionally well in Alsace and modern-day France, for our purposes we can call noble grapes fancy, fundamental, French grapes, while still having a place at the table in this section.

This noble grape Riesling has had a noble following since the 1400s and has migrated around the world. Unfortunately, in the United States in the late 1960s and early '70s, Riesling got a bad rep for being fruity and sweet and uncomplex. It's hard when a star falls from grace. Such is a candle in the wind—so delicate, personable, and so perceptible to ill will!

Riesling is unlike any other grape. I could write an entire book on Riesling (and many people have), and for still wines it would be important to discuss how terroir, region, and Riesling go hand and hand, but this is less relevant when bubbles get in the way.

What is important to understand is that Riesling has an incredible innate ability to create balance in a sparkling wine, with or without a dosage. (For more info about dosages, see page 41.)

When the Riesling grape is ripe, its own fruitand acid can be enough to make ethereal wines. If the wine needs more sugar, some winemakers will dose it with their own sweet, aged still Riesling Spätlese (fully ripe, late-harvest wine) or Auslese (a sweet-ripe, late-harvest wine produced by noble rot, or a gray Botrytis fungus).

Verband Deutscher Prädikatsweingüter
The VDP is a group of 197 winemakers and wineries who uphold a rigorous standard of quality.
To participate, a producer must abide by regulations dictating certain grape varieties for certain regions, harvesting by hand, production and pressing standards, and *méthode traditionnelle* fermentation.

The VDP uses very technical terms for their sparkling wines.

VDP.ORTSSEKT
Sparkling wine from village grapes

and

VDP.GUTSSEKT
Sparkling wine made from estate grapes.
Both of these mandate fifteen months ageing on lees.

VDP.LAGENSEKT
This top-tier sparkling is made from single vineyards and has to age for a minimum of thirty-six months on the lees.

NOW THE FUN STUFF: WEINS!!

RECOMMENDATIONS
Melsheimer Reiler Mullay-Hofberg Sekt 2015
Riesling
Mosel
Organic
Biodynamic

Schlossgut Diel Goldloch Riesling Sekt Brut Nature 2008
Riesling
Nahe
Sustainable

Peter Lauer Riesling Sekt 1991
Riesling
Mosel

Eva Fricke Brut Nature Rosé Pinot Noir 2016
Pinot Noir
Rheingau
Biodynamic

NOW TO AUSTRIA!
And Hungary, Czechia, and Turkey!

Austrian Sekt also has a PDO, or Protected Designation of Origin: Österreichischer Sekt mit geschützter Ursprungsbezeichnung. (Say that three times fast.)

As recently as 2016, the National Committee passed a proposal introducing a three-tiered system of Austrian Sekt.

Klassik
The grapes must be Austrian, but any form of production is allowed. There is a minimum ageing requirement of nine months on the lees.

Reserve
All the grapes must be Austrian and hand-harvested without machinery. The wine must be made *méthode traditionnelle* with a minimum of eighteen months ageing on the lees.

Grosse Reserve
The grapes must be hand harvested without machinery, from only one municipality, made *méthode traditionnelle* and aged on lees for a minimum of thirty months.

This recently developed system will help clarify what exactly is happening in the bottle!

RECOMMENDATIONS
Schloss Gobelsburg Brut Reserve NV
Pinot Noir, Riesling, and Grüner Veltliner
Niederösterreich, Austria
Sustainable

Something that fascinates me about Austrian wine is their appreciation for the ancestral method.

LET'S REVIEW.
Ancestral Method is old, like Larry King old, and yet still it charms everyone, just like Larry.

Ancestral method wines only have one fermentation.
These wines' fermentation can happen in a tank or in the bottle.
These wines are often created with organic or biodynamic practices.
These wines are often not disgorged.
These wines are often textural, yeasty, fruit forward. They can be funky and fun as hell.

Austria is such an amazing place, bordering on so many other countries: Germany to the northwest, Switzerland to the west, Italy to the southwest, Slovenia to the south, Hungary to the east, Slovakia to the northeast, and Czechia to the north. We don't think of Austria as the middle child, but just look at just the kinds of foods Austrians eat and you will see plenty of cultural overlap.

Austria's cuisine does very well with a light sparkling partner, and *pétillant-naturel*s have always had a tradition in the region. Recently some incredible producers have come onto the market.

Clause Preisinger St. Laurent 2016 Pet Nat
Burgenland
Sankt Laurent
Organic
Biodynamic
Sustainable

Franz Strohmeier Sparkling Rose NV
Steiermark
Weststeiermark
Biodynamic
No sulfites added
Czech ancestral method

Hungarian Pezsgő sparkling: Much of the sparkling wine in Hungary is produced using the Charmat or transfer method, although producers increasingly utilize *méthode traditionnelle*.

Milan Nestarec Danger 380 Volts 2017
Moravia, Czech Republic-
Müller-Thurgau, Neuburger, and Muscat
Natural AF

Királyudvar, Tokaji Pezsgő Henye 2013
Furmint
Tokaj, North Hungary
Biodynamic
Organic

Vinkara Kalecik Karasi Methode Traditionnelle 2014
Kalecik Karasi
Ankara, Turkey

ENGL

AND

England has a long history of consuming mass amounts of Champagne, but this country is less known for producing sparkling wine than for producing royal heirs, Downton Abbey, fish and chips, and the Spice Girls. In fact, I think no one says it better than Hugh Grant in *Love Actually:* "We may be a small country, but we're a great one, too. The country of Shakespeare, Churchill, the Beatles, Sean Connery, Harry Potter. David Beckham's right foot. David Beckham's left foot, come to that." So what I am trying to say is sparkling wine is not the first thing that comes to mind when you think of the UK because their (otherwise long) history is quite young in this department.

It takes a whole lot of money to start not only a wine region from scratch but a revolution in quality—especially for a wine that needs time. But money has been flowing into the region as producers recognize this new frontier's potential. With about two hundred active wineries in England in 2010, more than 3.5 million bottles were produced annually. Predictions point to nearly 10 million bottles produced by 2020, a crazy rapid expansion only possible in this newly developing market. Even large Champagne houses have bought property in England.

When I visited the UK on a whirlwind thirty-hour journey, two wineries were on my itinerary: Hattingly Valley and Nyetimber. In 2018, Hattingly clocked in at about 270,000 bottles a year, compared to one million bottled from Nyetimber the same year, which was a bountiful harvest. (Most years Nyetimber produces closer to six hundred thousand.) To put those numbers in perspective, many of the winemakers listed in this book produce about sixty thousand bottles a year! Lots of the quality-driven sparklings coming out of England are wines that are branded and, produced on a large scale, create a benchmark for the region through non-vintage wines.

I visited the south of England in the spring of 2019 and experienced firsthand the quality of English sparkling as well as the people starting a new dialogue around it. It's incredible to see a wine region that is still unknown and figuring it out—imagine exploring Kent, Sussex, Hampshire, and Cornwall (cutest names of wine regions ever) and talking to winemakers who are jazzed about sparkling wine.

The first vineyards strictly planted for sparkling began in the mid-1980s. The region had been known primarily for dabbling with German grape varietals that could withstand the colder climate of England and ripen enough for quality wine, until Nyetimber, one of the larger English sparkling houses, planted the Champagne trinity—Pinot Noir, Chardonnay, Pinot Meunier—in 1988 and pioneered producing *méthode traditionnelle*.

FRESH

The wines of England are characterized as FRESH. What does that mean?

I often taste in English sparkling wines a sugar-dusted, slightly under-ripe raspberry with lemon zest on the end, like a trifle or a soft baked torte with freshly whipped cream. Thirty years ago, before global warming began to accelerate, England's growing season was colder, and the wines were bracingly high in acid, sometimes thought of as austere and imbalanced. But as world warms, the wines in England could start getting a bit more heat during ripening season, with more sun exposure while grapes are on the vine. This could potentially soften out the acid found in these wines, giving way to riper fruit. Already the wines are starting to taste more broad and concentrated.

THE RULES FOR ENGLISH SPARKLING

England's PDO (Protected Designated of Origin), established in 2007, has rules that are not very strict.
*   All grapes must be from England.
*   The wine must be made in *méthode traditionnelle*.
*   Chardonnay, Pinot Noir, Pinot Noir Précoce, Pinot Munier, Pinot Blanc, and Pinot Gris are permitted.
*   Wines must be aged at least nine months on lees in the bottle.

Winemaking in England is evolving. Winemakers are working toward establishing a new set of rules and parameters on production and ageing to separate their quality wines from the masses. The region has been producing sparkling wine as long as I have been alive, and my growth is just beginning. In England, there is plenty to learn, an identity that has begun to solidify, and a beautiful future ahead for informed growth.

 RECOMMENDATIONS

Nyetimber Tillington Single Vineyard 2013
West Sussex
Pinot Noir, Chardonnay

Hattingley Valley Rosé
Hampshire, England
Pinot Noir, Pinot Meunier

Harrow & Hope Blanc de Blancs
Thames Valley
Chardonnay

At Nyetimber

In 2007, a Canadian couple made their way to England to try their hand at English sparkling wine, recruited by Nyetimber. Cherie Spriggs and her husband, Brad Greatrix, first set their sights on producing consistent sparklings for the house. Yet as she began to understand the diversity of terroir in her different parcels throughout Hampshire, Kent, and West Sussex, she began playing around with single-parcel single-vintage sparklings.

I tasted the 2013 Tillington Vineyard from West Sussex. Made from 80 percent Pinot Noir and 20 percent Chardonnay, this wine dripped with flavors of carob chocolate dipped in sea salt and perfumed with fresh roses. Cherie called it a Turkish delight.

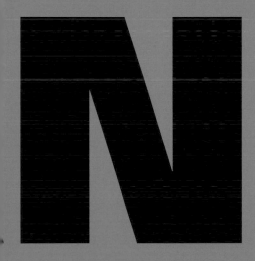

N

I fell in love with sake intellectually at first—its complicated process reminded me of Champagne's—and then through my palate. Champagne and sake have this in common: how they're made is hard as hell to understand. Sake production can be even more complicated than Champagne production, so when I first began learning about it, what quickly became clear to me was that an entire country's history of spirit production cannot be easily "summed up." To understand it fully takes a lifetime, much as sommeliers dedicate their lives to wine and its idiosyncratic intricacies. Nonetheless, I chose to include sake in our effervescent world tour, and I will do my best to make it digestible.

Hakkaisan, Sparkling Sake
Method Traditional
Chūbu

Sake starts with rice, not grapes. As a grain, rice has starch, which is a carbohydrate and glutinous—just to let you know this fun fact if you didn't already.

In case you think of sake more like a spirit, it's not. It's fermented and not distilled. Sake has a lower sugar content than wine, because it comes from rice not a grape. So pick your poison: carbs or sugar. (I am not writing a book about diets like Keto or Atkins or Paleo or Whole30, or whatever diet trend is popular in the future when you're reading this book—only pointing out this chemical difference.) Sake can have a much higher alcohol content than wine due to its unique fermentation process, so take note of this if you decide to switch to sparkling sake—I want to keep all my bubble babies out there safe.

To make sake, rice must be milled and polished. The categorizations of Junmai, Gingo, and Digingo refer to the amount of polishing a single grain of rice undergoes. But sake production not only takes into account different purity levels of rice but also the rice itself—its terroir and innate characteristics. (So not that different from grapes.)

The production of Sake is similar to wine fermentation. It only takes four elements to produce:
Rice
Water
Yeast
Koji (mold, yum!)

Rice gets steamed and cooled. Water, yeast, and *koji* are mixed together. When the rice is added into that mixture, *koji* jumpstarts the fermentation process, converting the rice's starch into sugar. The yeast then can eat away at the new sugars, converting them into alcohol.

It's a million times more complicated than this, but this is how Sake producers get the base, or "Sake Clair," which then can be processed using whatever method the producer chooses: the Charmat or tank method, force-carbonated in a tank, some *Pet-nat*, or maybe *méthode traditionnelle* with a second fermentation in the bottle!

Quality sparkling sake, relatively new to the market, used to be dismissed, considered a beverage for girlz. Seriously, this isn't a marketing ploy—it was produced for Japanese women, with fruit and sweeteners added. Now its popularity means large-scale institutional breweries all the way to small niche brewers produce interesting sparkling sakes.

 RECOMMENDATIONS
Hakkaisan Sake Brewery
Sake - Sparkling
Yamada Nishiki Rice
Chūbu

Fukucho
Sake - Sparkling
Nakateshinsenbon Rice
Chugoku

UNIT
STAT

ED
ES

Sparkling wine in the United States is a huge category to tackle. First of all, there are fifty states, and they all produce wine. While not all of them make sparkling wine, and while many of the states that do make sparkling wine don't have the climate to produce sparklers of real complexity, that's still a lot of geography to cover. United States sparkling history started in California, and it has since spread up and down the West Coast, into the middle of the country, down South a bit, and to the East Coast—predominantly in New York, my home state.

Clockwise from top left:

Ultramarine, Blanc de Noirs
Sonoma County, CA

Under the Wire, Sparkling Chardonnay Alder Springs Vineyard
Sonoma, CA

Cruse Wine Co., St. Laurent "Ricci Vyd" Carneros
Petaluma, CA

Caraccioli Cellars, Brut Cuvé
Carmel, CA

It's a New World, but there is both old and new thinking.

I won't be talking about Chandon or Domaine Carneros or Piper Sonoma or Roderer Estate. Most of these are owned by larger Champagne brands that decided to buy property in California in the 1980s as an investment, to produce *méthode traditionnelle* in a new territory. These are not the sparkling producers in America pushing the dialogue of unique sparkling. Branded, they truly are not much more than bubbles in a glass for when you need to pop some sparkling for a special occasion. Plus they aren't inexpensive, so for what you get I suggest you drink elsewhere.

Through my journey of effervescence, I have come to fall in love with American sparklings and feel a sense of pride for the bubbles being produced in the United States. Some are wildly fun and some are from places you never would expect. Some are traditional and a lot are pushing the boundaries with unique varietals and production techniques.

OLD/NEW

Some states are known for their viniculture. California, Oregon, and New York, for example, have dedicated wine regions where the terroir has been studied and documented for over eighty years, and the range of climates and subsoils provides opportunities for producers to try out varietals and see what will do well.

In states with cooler climates, you'll see more traditional Old World varietals from France and Italy, as well as noble varietals from Germany and Austria. In states with warmer climates, you'll see varietals that come from the southern parts of Old World regions as well as New World varietals. (It's not a universal rule, but many regions classified as New World tend to have warmer climates.)

Winemaking in the United States is still relatively new, and with this lack of old history comes plenty of learning curves. But this, along with relatively relaxed regulations in some states, allow for a lot of experimentation.

AVA

BUT FIRST, AVA (American Viticultural Areas)

There are no ageing requirements for sparkling in America, no rules about irrigating, and no varietal restrictions. The AVA system states that any region can claim AVA status if it uses up to 85 percent grapes or juice from that particular area. The only states that employ stricter regulations are Washington, for which producers need to claim 95 percent, and California, at 100 percent. The other rule is that when a specific grape is labeled, the wine must consist, at a minimum, of 75 percent of that grape.

The AVA system has everything to do with geography and nothing to do with winemaking rules, which is different from every other Designated Origin system. The upside is that producers have freedom to try anything, and the downside is that based on the label you, the wine consumer, will never quite know what you're going to get, unless it's explicitly stated.

SO WHAT SHOULD YOU DRINK FROM THE US OF A(IR)

SCHRAMSBERG

If I did have to name a sparkling winery that set the tone for American sparkling, it would be Schramsberg in Calistoga, California. The property was purchased over 150 years ago by Jacob Schram, a pioneer of vineyard cultivation in Napa. He was a wild fool at a time when spirits were the beverage of choice and growing grain would have made more sense. Almost one hundred years later, the winery was revitalized by Jack and Jamie Davies with the intention of making America's best sparkling wine, and the Davies family still runs the winery today. Their Blanc de Blanc was served at Nixon's 1972 "Toast to Peace" address and has become a government staple ever since. Schramsberg produces some of California's top *méthode traditionnelle* sparkling, and it is the brand that Californians love to boast about and the brand sparkling wine lovers respect.

ULTRAMARINE

I love Michael Cruse, aka the Petaluma Prince, who literally invented American wine drop culture with his highly coveted and allocated Ultramarine. People go gaga for this wine, made *méthode traditionnelle* and highly regarded by the Champenoise. When he and I were both in Champagne in 2018, we were introduced to each other by Fred Savart, one of Michael's besties and a wine producer influencer.

RECOMMENDATIONS CALIFORNIA

Caraccioli Cellars, Brut Cuvée 2013
Méthode traditionnelle
Chardonnay, Pinot Noir
Santa Lucia Highlands
Organic

Onward Wines 2018
Pétillant-naturel
Malvasia

POE Sparkling Rosé 2014
Méthode traditionnelle
Pinot Meunier, Pinot Noir
Napa Valley

Schramsberg Vineyards, Brut Reserve North Coast 2009
Méthode traditionnelle
Pinot Noir, Chardonnay
North Coast

Scholium Project, Blowout 2015
Force-carbonated
Lourreiro, Grüner Verdelho, Verdelho

Under the Wire, Alder Springs Vineyard 2015
Méthode traditionnelle
Chardonnay
Organic

Stolpman Vineyards, Combe Trousseau 2014
Pétillant-naturel
Trousseau
Ballard Canyon

Cruse Wine Co.
A slew of very cool sparkling wines made *méthode traditionnelle* including:

Valdiguié Rancho Chimiles 2018
Valdiguié or Napa Gamay
Sustainable
Organic

St. Laurent Ricci Vineyard Carneros, 2018
St. Laurent

ILLINOIS

Illinois Sparkling Company Brut Ombré Rosé
Méthode traditionnelle
Illinois-grown Chambourcin
Demi sec

MAINE

Oyster River Winegrowers, Morphos *Pétillant-Naturel* 2018
Pétillant-naturel
Cayuga White, Seyval Blanc
No sulfites added

NEW MEXICO

Gruet, Sauvage Rosé
Méthode traditionnelle
Pinot Noir

NEW YORK

Macari Vineyards, Horses Sparkling Cabernet Franc 2017
North Fork
Pétillant-naturel
Cabernet Franc

Wild Arc Farms
Hudson Valley
Piquette
Au natural

OREGON

Analemma, Blanc de Noirs 2014
Méthode traditionnelle
Pinot Noir
Columbia Gorge
Fifty-year-old vines

Gamine, Grenache Rosé Mae's Vineyard Applegate Valley 2018
Pétillant-naturel
Grenache
Applegate Valley

Roots Wine Co., Blanc de Noirs Red Hill Douglas County 2011
Méthode traditionnelle
Pinot Noir
Red Hill Douglas County
*A portion of the profits from all sales of ART BRUT wines is donated to the American Art Therapy Association

Soter Vineyards, Mineral Springs Brut Rosé Yamhill-Carlton District, 2013
Méthode traditionnelle
Pinot Noir, Chardonnay
Yamhill-Carlton District
Biodynamic

TEXAS

Southold Farm + Cellar 2018
Piquette

Château Frank, Blanc de Blancs 2012
Finger Lakes
Méthode traditionnelle
Chardonnay

Hermann J. Wiemer, Extra Brut *Méthode Champenoise*
Méthode traditionnelle
Riesling
Seneca Lake
Organic

VIRGINIA

Early Mountain Vineyards, *Pétillant-Naturel* Red 2018
Syrah
Pétillant-naturel

PIQUETTE

Piquette (French translation: "prickle") is a low-alcohol semi fizz that's made from the grape skins, seeds, and pulp that remain after the first round of wines is fermented. It was originally produced to satisfy (and inebriate) field workers. Inexpensive to produce and easy to drink, Piquette is becoming a bit of a trend for winemakers who want a more sustainable solution to winemaking. As a blend of whatever grapes have been pressed many times, there is often no clear *cepage* (in other words, no 50 percent one grape and 50 percent another). Often it's a mashup of many different parts of many different grapes jumbled together. Piquette amplifies a varietal's dominant tasting notes, enhancing but also simplifying the flavor profile.

GOIN
SOUT

There are some incredible *méthode traditionnelle* sparklers that come out of Australia, Tasmania, New Zealand, South Africa, and South America (grouped here because it's kind of down and under, and I have always been bad at geography) including unique bubbly that doesn't get imported to the United States. These are the sparkling wines that really excite me.

 **AUSTRALIA** Australia is known for the Shiraz grape, which screams 1970s housewife yet can be a real stunner—like a lot of those '70s babes. These sparkling reds can be everything from Grandma's deep, leather spice potpourri to fruit Bundt cakes. They can also range from affordable summer sippers to a solid price tag for vintage and old blended Shiraz. their abundance of fruit makes them amazing to cellar. You see, for wine, sugar is the elixir of life: when there is enough sugar remaining in the fruit, a wine can last in a cellar more than one hundred years.

 RECOMMENDATIONS
Seppelt Show Sparkling
Grampians
Shiraz

Best's Great Western
Victoria
Shiraz

 TASMANIA Tasmania is well known for its sparkling. Its cool maritime climate differentiates itself from the rest of Australia's wine regions and allows classic varietals like Pinot Noir, Chardonnay, Pinot Gris, Sauvignon Blanc, and Cabernet Sauvignon to ripen with richness and finesse, creating sparkling wines with balance and structure. As Tasmania is an island, the vineyards get huge gusts of salinic air, adding an elegant freshness to the wine. It's a challenging environment to work in, with producers having to protect their vineyards from strong winds coming off the Bass Strait, Indian Ocean, and the Tasmanian Sea. This area produces *méthode traditionnelle*, mainly with Pinot Noir and Chardonnay grapes.

 RECOMMENDATIONS
Henskens Rankin
Tasmania
Méthode traditionnelle
Pinot Noir, Chardonnay
Aged seven years on lees

NEW ZEALAND

New Zealand, the land of Sa-vi-B (totally street legal name for Sauvignon Blanc), for all my babes out there who are like, "I love Sauvignon Blanc all day, every day." I am going to blow your mind with two completely alternative Pét-Nat recommendations.

RECOMMENDATIONS
Orbis Moderandi
Sauvignon Blanc

Marlborough
Pétillant-naturel
Sustainable

Supernatural Wine Co.
Hawke's Bay, New Zealand
Sauvignon Blanc
Pétillant-naturel

SOUTH AFRICA

South Africa has a long tradition of producing inexpensive tank-fermented and force-carbonated sparkling wines. When seeking out bubbles from South Effrika (I love the accent so much), look for labels that have "MCC" (Method Cap Classique), which means *méthode traditionnelle*. Rules for MCC include a nine-month ageing on lees in the bottle so there is time for the wine to develop.

Many of these bubbly babies stay in South Africa, which is a heartbreak because they are amazing values for excellent, quality wines. You may have seen Ghram Beck, a large winery that produces the majority of what is known as SA sparkling. Its sparkling is made *méthode traditionnelle* with classic Chardonnay and Pinot Noir.

But I'm not here to romance what you know but rather offer you alternatives.

There are very special varietals like Chenin Blanc and other indigenous varietals that produce everything from elegant to totally wackadoo bubbly.

RECOMMENDATIONS
Mother Rock
Swartland
Pinotage, Colombard
Pétillant-naturel

Huis Van Chevallerie, Filia Chenin Blanc Brut Nature 2014
Swartlands
Chenin Blanc
Méthode traditionnelle

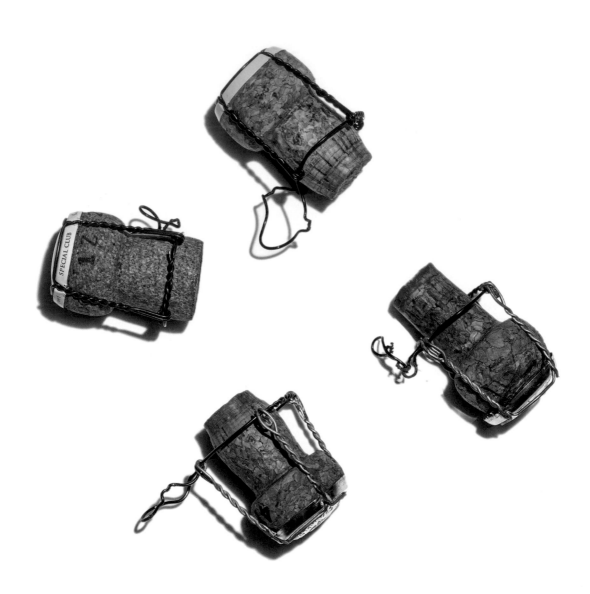

This New World wine region has been booming, with three places in particular getting into the game of sparkling wine: Argentina, Brazil, and Chile.

 ARGENTINA

Argentina is the largest South American producer of sparkling wine, with a large concentration in Mendoza, which is nestled nicely on the western foothills of the Andes. The climate is pretty perfect for sparkling with a high altitude and a desertlike growing season that makes for hot days and cool nights, ideal for a balance of acidity and fruit in the grapes. There is a wide range of grapes, but the majority of what I have seen is focused around more Old World varietals like Pinot Noir, Chardonnay, Chenin Blanc and Semillon, as well as Malbec for Rosé. Many of the wines, produced to be affordable and drunk young, are made using the Charmat, or tank method, but there are some good wines that are made *méthode traditionnelle*.

 RECOMMENDATIONS
Zuccardi Cuvée Especial
Blanc de Blancs Valle de Uco
Chardonnay
Mendoza, Argentina
Méthode traditionnelle

 BRAZIL

Brazil's main wine region is in the southern part of the country, in Serra Gaucha, which tends to be cold and wet with a high amount of annual rainfall. This is unique for a wine region because it makes the area constantly humid, raising the risk for fungal diseases. There's quite a lot of winemaking going on in Brazil because currently there's not a lot of oversight. Wine can be made in many different formats, labeled however it wants if it's not being exported, and can use unusual materials to dose such as cane sugar. One category that I think is audacious is Champagne, which includes a second fermentation in bottle or tank.

RECOMMENDATIONS
Família Geisse Brut
Chardonnay, Pinot Noir
Méthode traditionnelle

 **CHILE**

From north to south there is quite a diversity to the growing climate but across the board all the areas that grow sparkling do have a Mediterranean climate close to the Southern Pacific Ocean. With minimal rainfall, this region is lucky to avoid problems with disease and is able to preserve a fair amount of acidity in the wines.

RECOMMENDATIONS
Cono Sur Brut Valle del Bío-Bío
Pinot Noir, Chardonnay
Sur, Chile
Charmat, or tank method
Sustainable

ACKNOWLEDGMENTS

Thank you to my father, Federico Arce who has supported me throughout every venture I have ever dreamed of.

Thank you to my mother Susanne Buckler who knew I couldn't spell but thought I should write.

THANKS TO:
Noah Fecks Photography, Gary He Photography, Bridget Zhou Illustration, Indianna Hoover Illustration, Kristen Montenegro Design.

Models Hannah Houston, Austin Powers, Rachel Glickman, Amanda Fabian, Amelia Giordano, Amanda Stoffel, Kristen Montenegro, Sarah Krathen, Alana Zonan, and Michelle Doubble.

The teams of Air's Champagne Parlor, Niche Niche, Special Club, and Tokyo Record Bar in NYC.

My editor Caitlin Leffel

My art director Cristina Vásquez

My copyeditor Elizabeth Smith

Winemakers from Champagne and around the world for donating their time and product.

All the importers and distributors in NYC who continue to bring in the best sparkling wines from around the world.

My friends and family who support me.

FIRST PUBLISHED IN THE UNITED STATES OF AMERICA IN 2020 BY UNIVERSE PUBLISHING, A DIVISION OF RIZZOLI INTERNATIONAL PUBLICATIONS, INC.

300 Park Avenue South
New York, NY 10010
www.rizzoliusa.com

Principal photography by Noah Fecks
Portrait on pages 7-8 by Gary He.

Illustration by Bridgette Zou
Page 26 art designed by Kristen Montenegro.

Art Direction by Cristina Vásquez

Publisher: Charles Miers

Editor: Caitlin Leffel

Production Manager: Colin Hough Trapp

Managing Editor: Lynn Scrabis

Printed in China
2020 2021 2022 2023 / 10 9 8 7 6 5 4 3 2 1
ISBN: 978-0789339577
Library of Congress Control Number: 2020937361

VISIT US ONLINE:
Facebook.com/RizzoliNewYork
Twitter: @Rizzoli_Books
Instagram.com/RizzoliBooks
Pinterest.com/RizzoliBooks
Youtube.com/user/RizzoliNY
Issuu.com/Rizzoli

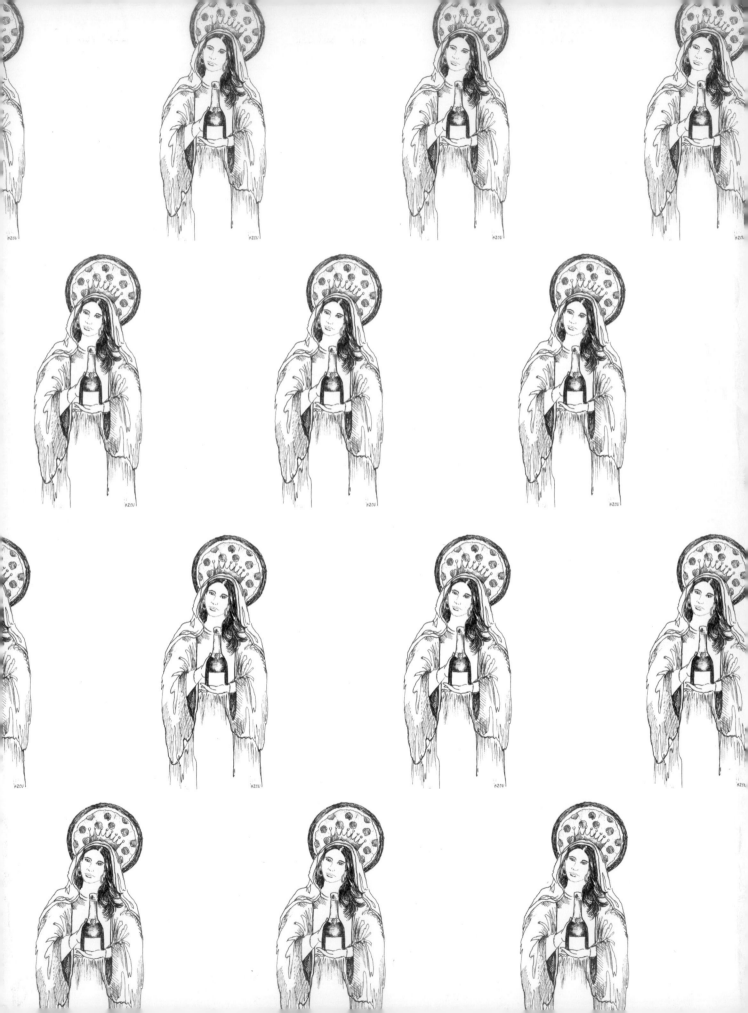